# LAKE VYRNWY

# LAKE VYRNWY

The Story of a Sporting Hotel

by

JOHN BAYNES

and

GEORGE WESTROPP

1992

First published in 1992 by
Sir John Baynes, Bt and G. V. Westropp

Available from Lake Vyrnwy Hotel
Via Oswestry, Mid Wales SY10 0LY

© Sir John Baynes, Bt and G. V. Westropp

Trade distribution by Kettering Books
14 Horsemarket, Kettering, Northants NN16 1DQ

ISBN 0 9519542 0 2

Printed by Villiers Publications,
26A Shepherds Hill, London, N6 5AH

# TABLE OF CONTENTS

Introduction by G. V. Westropp     xi

## Part I – How it Came About

Chapter 1   The Valley in the Days before the Lake    1
Chapter 2   The Creation of the Lake    7
Chapter 3   Building the Hotel    14

## Part II – A Century's Progress

Chapter 4   The First Half-Century — 1890-1940    21
Chapter 5   The Second Half-Century — 1940-1992    35

## Part III – The Sporting Side

Chapter 6   The Story of Trout Fishing on the Lake    51
            by G. V. Westropp
Chapter 7   How to Fish the Lake    67
            by G. V. Westropp
Chapter 8   The Shooting Rights    91

## Part IV – Some Personal Thoughts on Hotel Keeping

Chapter 9   Running a Sporting Hotel    117
Chapter 10   The Essentials of Hotel Management    124

## Appendices

Appendix A   Record of Trout Caught in the Lake from 1890 to 1991    130
Appendix B   Record of Game Shot    135

---

All chapters written by John Baynes except where shown to be by George Westropp

## LIST OF PLATES

*Facing page 46*
1. The Vyrnwy valley during the building of the dam
2. The hotel in about 1893
3. Miss Davies outside the hotel
4. A party of four guns and their ladies on the moor in about 1900
5. Major Lowndes and Miss Ruby Hill with fox-hounds in 1923
6. An aerial view of the hotel in 1928
7. Beaters on the moors in the late 1920s
8. The annual Boatmen's Fishing Competition in the 1930s

*Facing page 79*
9. Graham Martin in a butt on the grouse moors
10. Billy Thomas with the Rolls-Royce in 1939
11. Jamie Moir in 1953
12. Ruth Moir in 1953 with Benty, Sal, and her puppies
13. Michael Horton ledger fishing with Sim Carpenter
14. John Hill, farm bailiff
15. John Thomas, Ida Thomas, Alice Carpenter, and Miriam Probert standing outside The Tavern in about 1970
16. Bob Roberts, boatman
17. A group of motor-cycle enthusiasts outside the hotel in the 1930s
18. Members of The Tanners' Club about to set off from the hotel in 1991
19. Head keeper and three regular pickers-up

## LIST OF MAPS

| | |
|---|---|
| The General Location | vii |
| The Lake | x |
| The River | 87 |
| The Grouse Moors | 90 |
| The Pheasant Shoot | 98 |

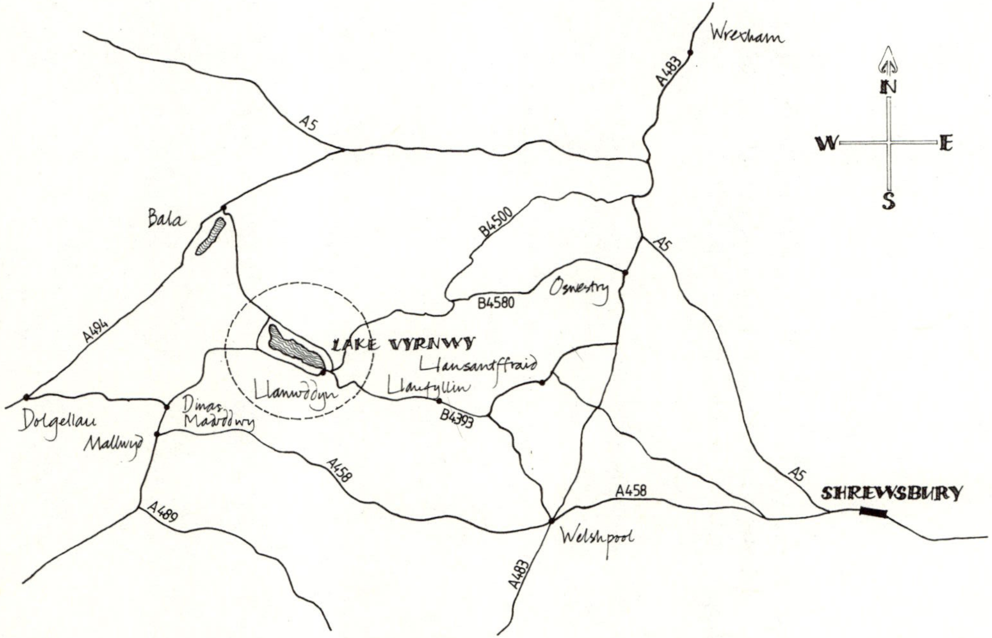

THE GENERAL LOCATION OF LAKE VYRNWY
SHOWING MAIN APPROACH ROADS

## DEDICATION

Dedicated to the staff of Lake Vyrnwy Hotel, both past and present, without whose courtesy and hard work it could not be the happy place it is, and always has been.

# ACKNOWLEDGEMENTS

We must start by paying tribute to the present management of the hotel for support in the preparation and distribution of this book. When Mr Jim Bisiker purchased Lake Vyrnwy Hotel in 1986 he formed a company called Market Glen to run it. He and his son Brian are on the board of this company, as are Mr Jim Talbot, managing director, and his daughter-in-law, Mrs Nikki Bisiker. These last two have been especially helpful and encouraging while the project has been in the process of completion. (Incidentally, John Baynes is a partner in a small way with Market Glen, retaining an interest in the sporting side of the business).

Many people have helped us to trace the story of the hotel through giving us their own personal reminiscences or putting us in touch with useful sources of information. We would like to thank Brigadier C. N. Barker, Mrs Ruth Druce, formerly Moir; M. J. Duggleby; Miss Ruby Hill; Ken Lloyd; Lieutenant-Colonel John Martin; Mrs Doris Moss; Brian Roberts; David Rowlands; John Thomas; Mrs Ida Thomas; Peter Sheen; and any other people we might have forgotten, to whom we extend our apologies for not mentioning them by name.

Several published books have been of particular importance, and these include the following: *Montgomery Collections*, Volumes VI and VII (1873 and 1874); *Wanderings with a Fly-rod*, by Sir Edward Durand (Herbert Jenkins, 1938); *Notes on Trout Fishing in Lake Vyrnwy and the Upper Vyrnwy River*, by R. E. Threlfall (1947); *Lake Vyrnwy and Around*, by W. M. Gallichan (1909); *History and Description of Llanwddyn and Lake Vyrnwy*, by D. W. L. Rowlands; *Angling Holidays in Pursuit of Salmon, Trout and Pike*, by C. W. Gedney (1893).

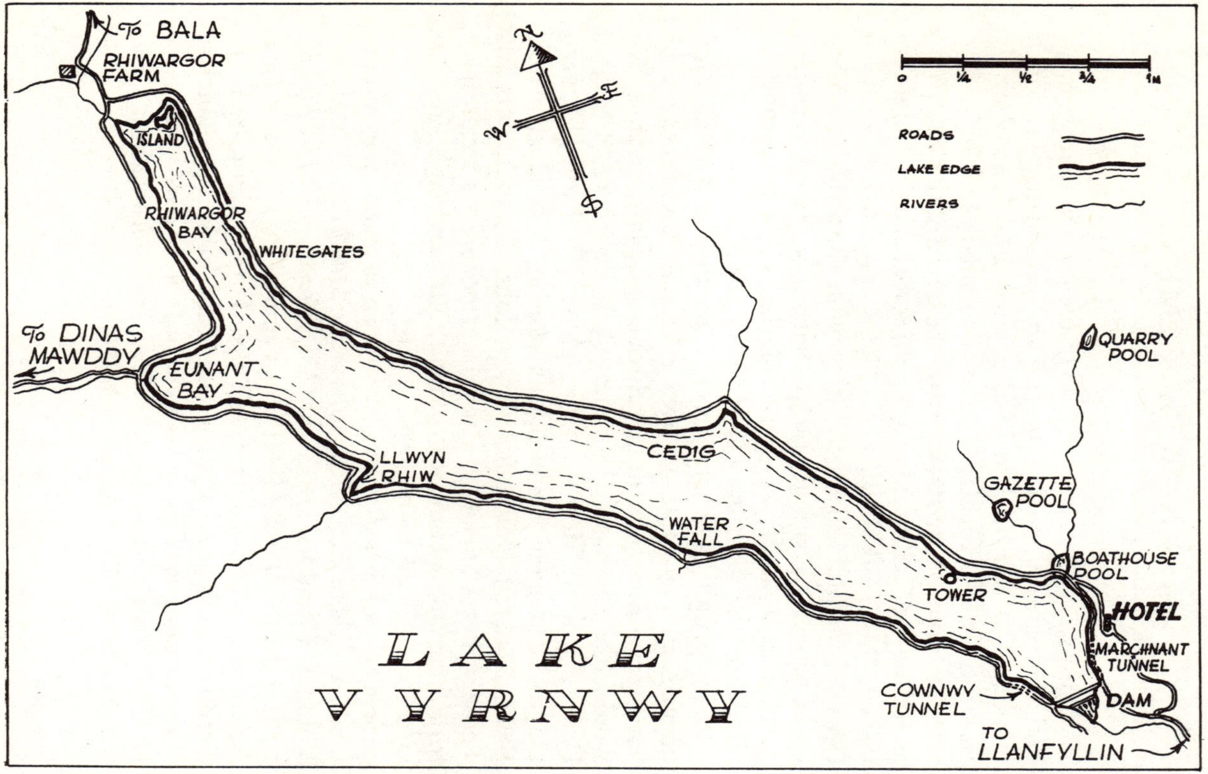
To BALA
RHIWARGOR FARM
ISLAND
RHIWARGOR BAY
WHITEGATES
To DINAS MAWDDY
EUNANT BAY
LLWYN RHIW
CEDIG
WATER FALL
TOWER
GAZETTE POOL
QUARRY POOL
BOATHOUSE POOL
HOTEL
MARCHNANT TUNNEL
DAM
COWNWY TUNNEL
TO LLANFYLLIN
N
E
W
S
0
1/4
1/2
3/4
1M
ROADS
LAKE EDGE
RIVERS
LAKE VYRNWY

# INTRODUCTION
## By G. V. Westropp

One warm afternoon in late May 1991, I sat in a boat pulled up on Mrs Morris's beach looking way down Lake Vyrnwy through the haze towards the Tower.

I started to muse on the massive endeavour to build the lake in the first place and the impact on an ancient and close knit community of being uprooted and transported down the valley below the dam.

I considered how much the hotel had changed in just my lifetime and all the different proprietors and guests coming and going over 101 years.

Countless thousands of fishers have drifted past that very beach in all seasons and weather over the century, while the moors and woods have echoed each year to the guns after grouse and pheasant.

Vyrnwy is a special place, I concluded, and it really was time for somebody to write a book about it all.

But, in fact, it was John Baynes who took the initiative. He called me about just such an undertaking a few months later, and we began the process which has lead to this publication.

For many, the Lake Vyrnwy Hotel is a second home and it has certainly been so for John Baynes and myself since the late 1940's.

We were both introduced to the lake by our fathers – Lieutenant-Colonel Sir Roy Baynes and Edward L. Westropp – in 1946. Indeed, John Baynes made Vyrnwy his actual home and ran the hotel in partnership with Mrs Ruth Moir (now Druce) between 1972 and 1987.

I cannot remember a time when I was not either looking forward to my next visit to Lake Vyrnwy or reflecting on one; whether a recent fishing trip or seeing-in yet another New Year at the hotel.

My visits have been so frequent over the years that I can

claim to have slept in every bedroom in the hotel and must know each rock and overhanging tree around the 12 miles shoreline of the lake.

In writing this book, we have sought to share our combined knowledge and experience of Vyrnwy over the years. We have also tapped the wisdom and insights of others who know the lake well, and have recorded them in our Acknowledgements.

My 1973 booklet on the fishing on Lake Vyrnwy included the following foreword by Sir Roy Baynes. The authors cannot think of a more suitable passage to introduce a book about the Hotel.

'After nearly fifty visits to Lake Vyrnwy, as one comes over the top of the hill above Llanwddyn, down round the hairpin bend, then up again to the lake, one finds the feeling of excitement and anticipation is as strong as ever. A short stop by the dam to see the water level and direction of the wind, and then on to the Hotel. Unpack, get into fishing clothes and out on to the lake to try and get an hour or so before it's time to come in for dinner. Then back to the Hotel to change, and before going into the dining room a little time in the Hotel bar, and a chance to look at the fish laid out on the trays in the hall. But why after so many years does one continue to look forward to it so much? First, of course, there is the fishing. This book will tell you all about that. Nowhere have I caught so many trout as I have at Lake Vyrnwy, but there is something more than that. Nowhere have I made so many friends, and nowhere can I be so sure of meeting them again, year after year. In the *Complete Angler*, Izaac Walton, when describing how to cook a pike with oysters and a variety of other succulent ingredients, wrote: "This dish of meat is too good for any but anglers and very honest men." I would para-phrase Izaac Walton and say – "Lake Vyrnwy is too good for any but anglers and very friendly men – women too, of course!"'

*Lieutenant-Colonel Sir Rory Baynes, Bt.,*
*Lake Vyrnwy, April 1973*

# Part I

## How it Came About

# CHAPTER ONE

## The Valley in the Days Before the Lake

In looking into the massive endeavour mentioned by George Westropp in his introduction, a start must be made with a short description of the valley before the lake was created. Fortunately a very active vicar was appointed to the parish of Llanwddyn in 1870, who busied himself collecting a mass of information about his parish and the village at the centre of it. In 1873 the Reverend Thomas H. Evans published his findings in Volume VI of the *Montgomeryshire Collections*, part of a great store-house of local history regularly produced from 1868 up to the present day.

As part of his description of the scenery, Evans quoted from an essay written by one T. W. Hancock, who from his narrative must have come to the valley from the north-west, following the road from Penybontfawr.

> 'At Abermarchnant the vale has the character of a pass, and is very contracted, in some places not more than a couple of chains lengths across, the hills on either side are pretty and well wooded. Near Cynonisaf [the farm on which the hotel now stands] it expands where a broad flat opens to view, which is bounded by the mountains of Eunant and Rhiwargor. The average width of the vale may be about three-quarters of a mile, and its extent about six miles. The flatness from the village to Eunant, to an eye untrained in observing natural beauties, would be uninteresting, on account of the morass-like nature of the ground, which is also broken up by many channels. But the tourist will be more than compensated when he enters the inlet by Rhiwargor, for here the scenery is at once changed as if by a magician's wand, and he is in the midst of scenery grand in point of colour, boldness, and breadth, and picturesque by its roughness and contrast of foliage and rock, cascade, etc.'

To this Evans added his own comment on the view to be obtained from the high ground above and to the west of Llanwddyn village:

> 'The scenery is not entirely confined to the upper end of the parish, for in standing on the north-east of St John's hill looking north, we find the beautiful little valley of Cedig, with all its variety of objects, spread before us, the hills on each side covered over with heather, and divided into kind of semi-circles by the green dingles and all the bright rivulets that pass along them, and nowhere can the eye be tired with sameness.'

Apart from the obvious absence of the lake, the main difference that an eye accustomed to the view of the area in modern times would notice would be the freedom of the hills from the great belts of conifers which now cover so many of them. The fields in the valley rose up to meet open heather moorland on all sides, and such woodland as existed was all broadleaf, mainly sessile oak. On the moors grouse were plentiful, while a wide range of birds were found on the lower ground. As well as all the more common small birds there were red kites and other raptors, and grey partridges were seen in the cultivated fields. Fish in the river were mainly trout and chub, with an occasional salmon.

Given the heavy annual rainfall in the area it is not surprising that there was everywhere an abundance of water, both flowing down from the hills in the streams, and filling the marshes along the course of the river Vyrnwy in the valley bottom. Evans reported that 'one third of the vale remained under water in the winter', and was useless for agriculture. The only crops this bog produced were rushes, interspersed with occasional alder and willow groves.

The village of Llanwddyn, which lay roughly half-way up the valley at the foot of the Afon Cedig, or Cedig river, took its name from an early Saint named Wddyn (pronounced 'Oothin') who was reported to have lived as a recluse in a nearby cave in the sixth century. Although the parish was also designated Llanwddyn, its church was named after St John of Jerusalem. The reason for this was that in the thirteenth century the manor of Llanwddyn had come into the hands of the Knights Hospitallers of St John, who had built a stone church in the village and dedicated it to their patron saint.

The parish of Llanwddyn, which extended over all the land to-day lying beneath the lake, plus the hills surrounding it, covered 19,500 acres. This was made up of 1,000 acres of cultivated land, 4,500 acres of meadow and pasture, 400 acres of woodland, and 13,600 acres of unenclosed common land. In 1873 it was divided into 50 holdings: 23 over 100 acres, and 27 under 100. The main owners of the land, other than common land, were the Earl of Powis, Sir E. Buckley, Bt, and Sir Watkin Williams-Wynn. Between them these three held just over 5,000 acres. Among other owners T. Storey had 422 acres, Thomas Gill of Cynonisaf 182, and Mary Erasmus of Allt-Forgan 175. The vicar's glebe extended to 73 acres.

At the time of the national census in 1871 the population of the parish was recorded as 443. 40 years earlier in 1831 this figure had been 668, or roughly one third greater. The lure of higher wages in the expanding industries of north-west England and the Midlands had drawn many people away from their isolated homes in the valley. To accommodate the population there were 37 houses in the village, and ten farmsteads in the surrounding countryside. Evans specifically mentioned 'four principal ancient houses' which he named Eunant, Rhiwargor, Gallt-Forgan, and Cynonisaf, stating that ' . . . these were occupied for generations by gentlemen having long pedigrees, and high standing.'

Farming was the main occupation of the inhabitants of the valley. Crops grown included barley and oats, a small quantity of wheat, potatoes, swedes and turnips. This was all for home consumption by the people themselves, or as winter feed for stock. In earlier times, when the population had been bigger, more land had been cultivated, but over the years it had been found easier and cheaper to turn land over to pasture for grazing. Some cattle were kept, but the main attribute for which the area was well known was the fine type of Welsh mountain sheep bred there.

For fuel the inhabitants relied largely on peat, which was

cut on the moors, and carted, or pulled on sledges, down to the houses in the valley. This simple self sufficiency was reflected in the diet of the majority of the people, which consisted of mutton broth, porridge, gruel, and milk. That such an apparently harsh way of life could be a remarkably healthy one can be demonstrated by the longevity of many of the inhabitants in days when the average expectation of life in the rest of Britain was far below what it is to-day. Evans reported 21 persons in the parish of over 75 years of age in 1870, of whom one was 102. Cases of others reaching 100 were recounted to him from previous years.

Like all communities in isolated rural areas at the time, the people of Llanwddyn retained many old superstitions and beliefs from far back in history. Fear of ghosts and evil spirits was still prevalent, heightened by the occasional appearance over the bogs by the river of a 'Will o' the Wisp'. This phenomenon is a light caused by spontaneous combustion of methane, or marsh gas, produced in water-logged ground. Primitive anxieties about the supernatural were somewhat at variance with the strong religious influences in the parish, there being three denominations of non-conformists with chapels in the village as well as the Church of St John.

Not many visitors came to Llanwddyn in the days before the lake was made. The few who did stayed in the Powis Arms hotel in the village, and were mostly men coming for the grouse shooting. One member of a shooting party, who had a very exciting experience while staying in the village, was a Mr Richard Blakeway-Philipps, from Hanwood in Shropshire. The newspaper report of the event is not dated, but since the Reverend T. H. Evans is mentioned in it, it must have been in the 1870s. The report tells how a 'water spout', or cloudburst, struck the valley, and in a few minutes the whole village was inundated.

> 'The school was completely isolated by the surging waters, and a number of the children who were in it were compelled to climb upon the forms and window sills to escape drowning. Throughout the village the greatest possible excitement prevailed, and the utmost anxiety was naturally felt for the safety of the children. Fortunately,

however, Mr Blakeway-Phillips of Hanwood, Shrewsbury, who happened to be staying at the inn, heard of the perilous position in which the little folks were placed, and he at once volunteered, if a rope could be obtained, to go to their rescue.

The current was flowing very rapidly, but he succeeded in crossing it. The landlord of the inn endeavoured to follow, but the rope broke, and he was washed back to the side from which he started. Upon reaching the school, which was surrounded by water to a depth of several feet, the gentleman broke open the windows, and with the assistance of a man who reached the school about the same time from another direction, the children were got out and taken to places of safety. A few minutes after the last child was removed, the building, which was erected on peaty soil, collapsed, and it was evident that had not assistance been very promptly rendered, all the children must have perished.

The many currents which rushed down from the neighbouring hills washed up the gravestones in the yard, and carried away several yards of the wall. Mr Phillips had to wait for upwards of an hour for the waters to subside before he could venture to return, and when he did so, the bridge over which he had crossed also gave way. The vicar of the parish, the Rev T. H. Evans, the schoolmaster, and the inhabitants of the village generally expressed their gratitude to Mr Phillips and others, who they felt had been first and foremost in rendering the assistance which proved so effectual.'

Isolated, peaceful, and rarely visited though it might still be as the 1870s progressed the upper Vyrnwy valley was, by virtue of its shape and geological base, of interest to a distant body of people who were, before long, to make a massive impact on the lives of all who lived there. This body was the City Council of Liverpool, and the concern of its members was to find a site for a new reservoir to provide more water for the ever expanding population of the great, sprawling urban area they controlled along the banks of the Mersey.

Various sites were under consideration in northern England-

and Wales, but in most cases some snag prevented them from being suitable. In the summer of 1877 Mr Deacon, the city engineer of Liverpool, arrived in Llanwddyn to investigate the possibility of damming the river Vyrnwy at a point somewhere below the village to create a large, artificial lake capable of holding many millions of gallons of water. During his surveying of the area a rock bar was discovered lying across the bed of the valley, at the point where it began to narrow two miles south of the village. The potential of this rock bar as a base on which to construct a dam convinced Deacon that he had at last discovered a good site for the creation of a reservoir.

# CHAPTER TWO

## The Creation of the Lake

To make it clear why Mr Deacon was investigating the possibility of building a dam in the valley of the river Vyrnwy it is necessary to explain briefly the problems of the city of Liverpool in obtaining enough water for its ever increasing population. What had been a small town at the beginning of the eighteenth century had become by the middle of the nineteenth a sprawling city with administrative responsibilities not only for Liverpool and Bootle, but for such areas as Crosby, Aintree, Kirkby, Huyton, and Halewood: in fact for the whole of north Merseyside. By the 1840s the water supply had become totally inadequate, so in 1847, following an Act of Parliament, a large reservoir was constructed 28 miles away at Rivington in Lancashire, from where water was piped to the city. Further small reservoirs were built in the following years, but by 1865 the increase in demand had overtaken the capacity of the new supplies. Public health had much improved when the water from Rivington had first became available, but as the demand once again exceeded supply a general deterioration in health was noted. By 1866 it was clear that a new source of water had to be found.

Mr Duncan, the city engineer, reported on a number of sites for the construction of a new reservoir in the Lake District and north Wales. He personally favoured a scheme involving Lake Bala and the river Tryweryn, which joins the river Dee just below it. Matters were then delayed by Duncan's death. The construction of a new railway caused Mr Deacon, his successor, to report in due course that the Bala scheme was no longer possible. Consideration was given in 1874 to more schemes in Lancashire and the Lake District, but it was not until 23 July 1877 that Deacon was instructed to report on the possibilities of the Vyrnwy valley.

In contrast to the rather dilatory approach to the problem of the preceding eleven years, Deacon now worked more swiftly, and presented his report on 27 November that year. It was accepted in principle, and in September 1878 trial shafts were sunk at the chosen site to see if the rock bed would provide a secure enough foundation on which to build a dam destined to hold back a head of water of ten thousand million gallons.

In 1880 the Liverpool Corporation Waterworks Act was passed by Parliament, and received the Royal Assent on 6 August. Preparations were at once put in hand to gather the work-force and equipment necessary for the construction for what was to become the first large masonry dam in Britain, and the largest artificial reservoir in Europe at the time. Work on the site began in July 1881, commemorated by a stone laid at the northern end of the dam on 14 July by the Earl of Powis. This can be seen to-day, along with two others commemorating later stages of the work.

The stone for the masonry was obtained from the quarry specially opened up in the valley on the eastern side of what is now the lake, the road to which branches right at the bottom of the hotel drive. All other materials were brought by horse and cart from the railway station at Llanfyllin, ten miles away. Stabling for up to 100 horses was built in Llanfyllin, where parts of the walls can still be seen, and at Llanwddyn. The road between the two places had to be improved, and at one point realigned to ease the gradient. The labour force topped 1,000 men at the busiest stage of the work on the dam. Many of them were stone masons working in the quarry, dressing the stone which was not easy to handle.

In a remarkably short time, compared with that taken to reach a decision to build it, work on the dam was completed. The old village of Llanwddyn, and all buildings in the valley that were due to be covered by the water of the lake, were demolished. A new church, dedicated to St Wddyn, had been built on a rocky spur of the hill on the north side of the new works. On 27 November 1888 this new church was consecrated, and the next day the valves at the base of the dam were closed. To general surprise the new lake filled more rapidly than anticipated, and just under a year later, on

22 November 1889, the water flowed over the lip of the dam.

On the same hill as the church a monument was erected in memory of ten men who were killed during the course of the building works, presumably due to accidents on the site, and a further 34 who died from other causes while construction was in progress. Given the average expectation of life for a manual labourer in those days this is not a surprising figure for a seven year period.

The building of the dam was not the only engineering feat necessary for the provision of a water supply: equally vital was the creation of a suitable means of bringing it to Liverpool. The water's 68 mile journey to taps in the city started at the straining tower, designed to both strain it through huge, wire-gauge filters, and to regulate the level of draw-off. From the tower, which is so often compared to a castle on the Rhine, and is such a well known feature of the Vyrnwy scene, it passed to the start of a tunnel driven two and a quarter miles up through the hillside in a north-easterly direction. Into the tunnel was placed a 42-inch pipe. Along the route to Liverpool of this massive pipe, capable of carrying thirteen millions of gallons a day, balancing reservoirs and filtration works were set up. On 14 July 1892 the first water flowed into the city.

Over the following years further steps were taken to increase the amount of water that could be drawn off the lake. By 1905 a second line of 42-inch pipe had been laid. A third was added in the 1920s and 30s. To augment the flow of water into the lake itself, diversion dams were constructed in the beds of two streams which flow into the river Vyrnwy below the dam: the Marchnant on the north side, and the Cownwy on the south. From the small lakes created by these dams, tunnels were driven down to carry extra water into the lake. The Cownwy tunnel comes out on the southern shore opposite the hotel, and at times of heavy rain can be seen pouring out a huge, foaming torrent into the lake. The completion of these works in 1910 was marked by an official opening by the then Prince of Wales, later King George V, and the planting of a tree which can be seen on the right of the road just beyond Pont Cynon, better known to visitors as the 'boat-house bridge', lying at the bottom of the hotel drive.

A further building task was called for in the re-housing of the people whose homes had disappeared under the waters of the lake. In keeping with the quality of the dam, fine, solid, stone houses were erected on either side of the valley immediately below it, and these can still be seen and admired a century later. Although there were at the time, and have been since, many people who have criticised the decision to flood the valley, the lake's creation has in fact brought prosperity and stability to the area. During its long period of guardianship up to 1973, when the estate was passed into the hands of the Severn-Trent Water Authority, the Liverpool Corporation proved to be a model landlord and employer. A clue to the benefits of this good care of the community can be demonstrated by the fact that the census of 1961 showed a population fall of only ten percent from the 1871 figure, while the average drop in seven similar parishes in the surrounding area was 50%.

While construction work was in progress housing was required for the workmen on the site. Dr Hugh Jones, one-time surgeon to the Corporation, recorded in 1893 that '. . . two series of semi-detached wooden huts were erected, each but consisting of a large living room, a store room, two small bedrooms, and a sleeping apartment for twelve men'. Although intended as purely temporary accommodation, some of these huts were still occupied by local people, who had moved into them, long after the dam had been completed.

In order to avoid disrupting the flow of the river Vyrnwy below the dam, arrangements had to be made to allow water to pass through valves at its base into the bed of the river. As well as the regular daily discharge, on four days a month, for eight months of the year, a big head of what was termed 'compensation water' was released into the river. The thrust of both these types of discharge passing through relatively narrow valves was so great that a decision was made to employ it to make electricity. A generating plant was installed in 1902, which continued to supply Llanwddyn village, the Corporation offices, and the hotel with electricity until 1960, when Manweb brought a mains supply to the valley.

The enterprise of providing Liverpool with water

embraced another whole range of responsibilities beyond the physical creation of the reservoir and the pipe lines leading from it. This was the purchase and management of land: both the land that was to be flooded, and also an extensive area forming the watershed which would drain into the new lake. To have full control of the watershed was especially vital in view of the intention that Vyrnwy should be a clean water reservoir, from which the water would flow untreated, except for normal filtration, directly into taps in Liverpool.

There is not space here to give more than the briefest account of the various stages in the process of purchasing the land which eventually made up an estate of 26,000 acres. Initially 13,415 acres were purchased out of a catchment area of 18,260. In due course the rest of the land in the catchment came into the hands of the Corporation. When the Marchnant and Cownwy diversionary dams and tunnels were built, more ground was bought up. A last purchase of some land in 1930 brought the estate to its present size. The main sellers were the major landowners mentioned earlier in Chapter 1. The Earl of Powis retained the sporting rights over all the land he sold, as did Sir Watkin Williams-Wynn over part of the grouse moors in the parish of Llangynog. Mr Thomas Gill of Cynon Isa used the money he received to extend his other house, called Brynderwen, lying 12 miles away near Llanfyllin. It was on Thomas Gill's land that the hotel was in due course built.

Management of the estate during the early years was in the hands of Mr W. Forrester Addie of Welshpool, who was also agent for the Powis estates. The first resident agent at Vyrnwy was appointed in 1928. This was Mr Humphrey Howard, who remained in office for 36 years, until retiring in 1964. A man of great ability and character, as well as possessing a fine sense of humour, Humphrey not only became 'uncrowned king' of Vyrnwy, but was for many years an important figure on the county council, first of Montgomeryshire, then Powys. In 1959 his step-son David Rowlands joined him as an assistant, following him as chief agent on his retirement. In 1979 David left to run his own farm, and Mr Michael Duggleby, the present incumbent, took up the post.

In a useful short book entitled *History and Description of Llanwddyn and Lake Vyrnwy*, from which much of the material for this chapter has been drawn, David Rowlands has described how the Corporation ran the estate, and how the afforestation of the land around the lake took place:

'The estate as purchased consisted almost entirely of tenanted farms more than two thirds of whose land was unenclosed mountain. Between 1890 and 1912 the Corporation planted about 900 acres with mainly coniferous plantations although in many areas about 10% of beech were included as a soil improver. During that period the Corporation were advised that it would be desirable to plant the slopes surrounding both the lake and the lower parts of the main feeder streams, and in 1912 they entered into an agreement with the Development Commissioners to plant a further 4,000 acres. The First World War delayed the start of the additional planting but in 1920, in conjunction with the Forestry Commission, which had succeeded the Development Commissioners, work began.

Farms were taken in hand by the Corporation as and when they became vacant; the plantable land was planted and the mountain land was merged with farms managed by the Corporation. By 1936 the planting programme was completed and the Corporation were farming about 11,000 acres of which all but 600 acres were mountain land.

During the war of 1939–45 the country was desperately short of timber and much of the original 900 acres of the Corporation's plantations were felled, about 60,000 tons of timber being produced from the estate during the war.'

What was left of the 900 acres of the Corporation's own plantations was sold in 1946 to the joint scheme with the Forestry Commission, and so became included with the 4,000 acres under that shared control. The money raised was used to build the community centre, school, and village known as Abertridwr, the extensive and well designed buildings of which are seen on the right of the road, soon after coming into the valley, on rounding the hairpin bend on the road from Llanfyllin.

All that remains is to round off this chapter with a brief updating on the situation in 1992, at the time of writing. Following the Water Act of 1974, Lake Vyrnwy and the estate passed from the control of Liverpool Corporation into that of the Severn-Trent Water Authority. So that the water could continue to be used by Liverpool, an abstraction licence was granted to the North-West Water Authority, which now looks after the city's interests, enabling it to draw off from the lake. The management of the estate has not changed in principle since the Severn-Trent Water Authority took over, and it is still looked after by a resident agent occupying the long established offices at the south end of the dam. In practice there have been some considerable alterations to the old, paternal Corporation style of operation. The workforce on the estate has been very greatly reduced, and much foresty work is now done by contractors, as opposed to the home based forestry gang. Another major change in practice came in the mid-1980s, with the start of a policy of allowing the sale of houses and buildings to private purchasers: something always resisted fiercely by the Corporation. This change of policy has had an important influence on the history of the hotel.

## CHAPTER THREE

## Building the Hotel

The decision to build a hotel beside the lake was a natural development of the intention to create a new reservoir in an isolated valley 68 miles from Liverpool, and ten miles from the nearest rail-head. The site made it difficult for anyone wishing to spend any length of time in the area of the lake to do so without finding overnight lodging. The requirement for a hotel became obvious soon after the enterprise was launched. Before describing the categories of visitors expected to make use of it, it must be stressed how excited many people were all over Britain, as well as in other countries, at the news of the setting up of this massive engineering project. From the start it was clear that it would draw sightseers and other viewers in considerable numbers.

The first category of anticipated visitors comprised the members of the Liverpool Corporation, and other dignitaries from the city. To ensure that there would be rooms available for city councillors and officials when required, conditions were written into the terms of the lease of the hotel which stipulated that accommodation had to be reserved for them at certain times of the year. Category two consisted of a wide range of people, mainly engineers, who were known to be interested in the construction of the dam, and the method of drawing water from the lake. Both during the construction phase, and long after the valley had been flooded, experts came from all over the world to study the techniques used in creating what was then, and for a long time, the biggest artificial lake in Europe.

The third category of visitors for which the hotel was built embraced a variety of private people, including those who would be coming to fish or shoot, walkers, naturalists, artists, and ordinary holiday-makers. Given the social conditions of the time these early customers with sufficient money and leisure to spend several days or weeks at a spell away from home could be expected to require good, spacious accommodation, and in many cases to bring their own personal servants with them.

The site first chosen for the building of the hotel was high on a hill at the northern end of the lake, directly above the house and farm at Rhiwargor. It would have been a magnificent setting with splendid views, but had to be abandoned for an important but prosaic reason. Since the aim was to preserve the water in the purest possible form, no sewage was permitted to find its way into the reservoir. From the rocky hillside where the hotel might have been erected no suitable way could be found of directing the sewage away from contaminating the lake, and there was no possibility of siting a septic tank or filtration plant. Another site had to be found.

The place finally selected to erect the hotel provided almost as good a view of the waters as the original choice, and had three further advantages. It was easier of access; the sewage could be taken away via filter beds to a stream joining the river Vyrnwy below the dam; and finally it was in a drier area. Surprisingly, the rainfall at the northern end of the lake, due to the surrounding hills, is ten or more inches higher than at the south in an average year.

As can be seen from one of the illustrations, the original building was smaller than the one that stands to-day. Looking at the photograph dated *circa* 1893, the two lower, rather shed-like structures beyond the main hotel housed the kitchen and usual domestic offices and stores. Beyond them again, the stone coach-house with a pinnacle on top also contained the farm bailiff's quarters. Further on, out of sight, were cow sheds and some excellent stabling, with four good loose boxes as well as stalls and a tack-room. Although apparently well set up with all the varieties of accommodation and working areas required, it was not long before, as is so often the case with new places, these were found inadequate.

About the turn of the century several cottages were erected. The best of these was a neat stone house, set in a secluded spot about 100 yards north-east of the hotel, which became known as the 'Eagle's Nest'. It still stands to-day, and is occupied by Mr Peter Talbot and his wife. A row of four other workmen's cottages were erected at the far end of the field above the hotel, where there are now some sheep pens. These were later pulled down. The tenants found it necessary to put up a number of wooden buildings as well, mostly connected with the farm and the sporting facilities, which included extra cow houses, a gun room, overflow accommodation for servants, and a laundry. Another slightly surprising outbuilding to find in the grounds was the local post office, which was sited on the lawn just opposite the side entrance to the main hotel.

In 1905 a major reconstruction of the main building was carried out. The early kitchen block was pulled down, and a long wing was added, stretching up towards the farm area. On the ground floor a new kitchen and ancillary rooms were placed on one side of a central corridor: on the other was a large billiard-room and a steward's room, occupying what is now the restaurant. Upstairs there were two floors of living accommodation adding approximately 19 letting bed-rooms to the 15 in the earlier part of the building. (In time this number would be increased, as private sitting rooms were converted to bed-rooms.) From 1905 to 1930 the exterior of the hotel remained looking much the same as it does in the photograph, among the illustrations, taken from the air by Graham Martin in 1928.

1930 saw the erection of a further extension at the end of the new wing. This added two bed-rooms and a bath-room upstairs, and a steward's room and staff room below. At this point the billiard-room disappeared, allowing it and the earlier steward's room to be opened up into one large dining-room. The rooms which had earlier been used as dining-rooms were redesignated drawing-room and smoking lounge. There were still only a few bath-rooms in the hotel, and hot water was carried to the bed-rooms morning and evening by the chamber-maids in brass cans. Chamber pots were still in regular use in the bed-rooms, and the unfortunate chamber-maids had the task of 'slopping' them out in the mornings.

Although the outer structure of the buildings was not greatly altered for the next 60 years, there were constant internal changes. In the late 1940s hot and cold running water was piped to wash-hand basins in all bed-rooms. One elderly permanent resident was so annoyed by this modern 'fad' that he departed, complaining bitterly at not having his brass can of hot water brought to his room. In the 1950s four extra private bath-rooms were provided, to make a total of six bed-rooms with this increasingly demanded facility, to which were added a further five in the 1970s. In 1956 a major alteration to the tap-room, or public bar, was put in hand. Up to that year it had been lodged in a fairly small and not very comfortable room at the back of the 1930 extension. To provide better premises, the building occupied by the farm bailiff's quarters and a coach-house was taken over, and what amounted to a separate local pub was created, with a spacious public bar and a smaller lounge bar overlooking the lake. Further improvements were made in the 1970s and early 80s, with cooking facilities and a pool-room added to what was now referred to as 'The Tavern', rather than 'the tap-room'.

The circumstances by which the hotel freehold was purchased by the sitting tenants in 1985, and sold by them to the present owners soon afterwards, is explained in a later chapter. The result was that the building was subjected to massive internal alterations in 1987, which are being followed by further developments at the time of writing in 1992. This next round of changes will alter, and hopefully improve, certain aspects of the outside appearance of the hotel, especially in the region of 'The Tavern' and the present garages.

The recent work done in the building has been necessary to keep pace with changes in demand among potential customers. To-day a private bath-room with each bed-room is considered essential in any good class hotel, while 100 years ago affluent guests regarded private sitting-rooms as more important. As the years have gone by the changes in taste among visitors has caused the structure of the hotel to be altered to suit them. What is unchanging, and perhaps its greatest asset, is the superb panorama of lake and hills which can be seen from its windows: a view which never fails to give pleasure whatever the mood of the weather.

## Part II

*A Century's Progress*

# CHAPTER FOUR

## The First Half Century, 1890–1940

The first tenant to take a lease of the newly built hotel in 1890 was Mr G. Ward. The Liverpool Corporation was lucky to find a man who was clearly of considerable wealth, since he took over an empty building, which he had to furnish and set up with all fittings, other than those fixed fittings which were part of the premises. His outlay was £7,000 on all these items, which in 1992 terms would be approaching £280,000. No doubt he was charged a low rent, but with no established goodwill to go with the business, this would be the only advantage in taking the place from a commercial angle. However, it would seem that Ward was as much interested in the sporting rights offered with the lease as in the hotel itself. Evidence of this, as will crop up again in a later chapter, can be found in the details of the first year's fishing on the lake in 1891, which show him to have been the most successful, individual fisherman of the season. To have time to pursue his own sporting interests he employed a Mr W. Durant Gibbings to manage the hotel for him, which was a considerable luxury in an establishment with only 15 letting bedrooms, of which an unusually high proportion were singles. Before long the financial strain proved too much for him, and Ward decided to move on, contriving to assign his lease to Miss Davies in 1892 or 93, but suffering a loss of several thousands during his short, if pleasant, stay at Lake Vyrnwy.

Miss Davies was to remain at Vyrnwy for very much longer, though in the end to have had little more financial success than her predecessor. She was a very capable woman, who ran a very comfortable hotel with a reputation for good food. Much of her trade came from visiting engineers and reporters for technical journals, who, in the early years, were constant arrivals to examine the wonders of the new dam and lake. There were also figures from the Corporation to be put up during their frequent inspections of the new works. Private people usually came for longish visits of up to a fortnight. Complete families often arrived, bringing their own personal servants. It can be assumed that the small bedrooms on the second floor were designed to be used by children and servants, while the parents had bed-rooms and sitting rooms on the first floor. A diary dated 1896, discovered in the attic not long ago, showed relatively few bookings, but nearly all for longish visits.

No doubt with Miss Davies's full approval, and perhaps at her instigation, a new wing was added to the hotel in 1905. This made it a more potentially profitable size, adding a further 19 bedrooms to the original 15. Unfortunately this addition was of little benefit to Miss Davies, who found the necessary outlay on equipping and furnishing the extension a serious drain on her resources. Within a few years she was anxious to surrender her lease, having for some time been trading at a loss. She attempted to sub-let the hotel, but found no takers. Eventually, in 1909, a Mr William Hampson arrived on the scene, and it is from studying his correspondence that much of the story of these early days has been pieced together.

By trade Hampson was a manufacturer of leather goods, owning a factory largely devoted to making harness and equipment for horse drawn vehicles, still very much in demand until well into the twentieth century. His venture into the hotel business made him the proprietor of the inn at Pen-y-Guryd, a well known resort of mountain climbers in those days, as it still is now. Both at Pen-y-Guryd and Vyrnwy he employed managers to run the hotels for him, in the latter case a Mr Bennett. While taking a keen interest in both establishments, he was often away from them, staying at the house he owned at Bettws-y-Coed. When he moved from Pen-y-Guryd he brought with him, to run the home farm as working bailiff, John Hill, the father of a large family, many of whom still live in or near Llanwddyn. Eventually there were nine Hill children, five girls and four boys. The family lived in the farm bailiff's house, which is to-day the site of The Tavern, the pub next to the hotel.

Several of the children were to work in various capacities for the hotel as they grew up. Ruby, the eldest, was in charge of poultry and the dairy for many years, while Ida and Gwen became chamber-maids: Ida for nearly 60 years. Teddy was for a time a chauffeur and driver, and Harry worked on the farm as a shepherd. Sammy followed his father as farm bailiff for a time, and Joan worked in the bar during World War II.

Hampson negotiated a limited ten year lease on taking over in 1909. In view of what he knew of the financial problems of his two predecessors this was wise. He had discovered, to use his own words, that:

> 'The first lessee, Mr Ward, lost a good many thousands in a few years. Miss Davies, after running the place many years died very poor. If she had not obtained a good price for the goodwill of the lease she would have been insolvent. She had been trading at a loss for some years when I took the business over.'

The actual amount Hampson paid Miss Davies for the lease was £2,400, approximating to £85,000 to-day.

During his first five years at Vyrnwy, Hampson, who was clearly an efficient businessman, managed to make a profit. In 1913 the gross profit was £1,552, leaving £1,168 (say £40,000 to-day) after writing off depreciation of the lease, furniture, and other items.

When the First World War started his fortunes changed. By 1918 he was greatly concerned with the matter of who would take on the lease which he was due to surrender the following year, it being important to him that the newcomers were financially strong enough to pay a good price for the goodwill of the business, the tenants furnishings and fixtures, and several wooden buildings in the grounds. These buildings included the wooden house he had erected himself for his own use, 100 yards from the hotel beside the back drive, at a cost of £750. Now known as 'The Cottage', it is the home of the general manager and his family.

Throughout 1918 Hampson was in constant correspondence with Mr W. Forrester Addie, the agent for the estate, and Lieutenant-Colonel J. R. Davidson, DSO, the Liverpool

Corporation Water Engineer, on the subject of the new tenants. The hotel was advertised in several journals and newspapers in early June 1918 in the following terms:

'SPORTING ESTATE AND HOTEL,
LAKE VYRNWY, NORTH WALES.

Owing to the Expiration of lease the first-class hotel belonging to the Liverpool Corporation at Lake Vyrnwy, with farm and extensive fishings, general shootings, and grouse moors, will be to LET from Lady Day, 1919. Tenders are invited for a Lease of the whole of the property or separate tenders for: (a) The Hotel, the farm, the fishing over the reservoir, tributary streams, and River Vyrnwy, and the general shootings; (b) the grouse moors. THE HOTEL stands at a height of 1,000ft. above sea level and commands a view of lake and mountain scenery of unsurpassed beauty. The Hotel contains 40 bedrooms, with private and public sitting rooms, bathrooms on all floors, a fine billiard room with lavatory attached and all modern conveniences. The buildings is lighted throughout by electricity. It is surrounded by attractive walks and drives through mountain and sylvan scenery. Connected with the Hotel are a garage, with separate stalls for five cars, stables, coach-house and the usual offices. Close to the main building there is a post and telegraph office with residence for the Postmaster. There are also conveniently situated five recently built workmen's cottages. A BUNGALOW of modern construction with eight bedrooms may be included in the letting. Distance to the Hotel from Penybontfawr Station (Tanat Valley Ry.) eight miles, from Llanfyllin Station ten miles, from Chester 38 miles, and from Shrewsbury 30 miles. A FARM of about 500 acres, with necessary outbuildings, is Let with the Hotel. THE FISHING includes extensive rights over Lake Vyrnwy and its tributary streams and over a length of the River Vyrnwy. The lake is the largest sheet of water in Wales, five miles long and twelve miles around on good level roads. Its high reputation for trout fishing is well known to anglers. There is a boat-house for sixteen boats.

THE GENERAL SHOOTINGS embrace all the lands and woods owned by the Corporation in the Vyrnwy Catchment area of 18,000 acres (except the grouse moors). The grouse moors include four moors, having a total area of 6,000 acres well stocked and convenient of access.—For further particulars and orders to view apply to Messrs. ADDIE & SONS, Welshpool; or to the TOWN CLERK, Liverpool. Tenders must be sent in, in a sealed envelope endorsed "Lake Vyrnwy Hotel", addressed to the Town Clerk, Municipal Buildings, Liverpool, by not later than noon on Monday, July 1st, 1918.'

To some extent these advertisements were a waste of money, since in the end the lease was taken up by a syndicate of three members – Mr Caley, Mr Carkeet James, and Major Lowndes – who had been expressing an interest in it well before any advertising was put in hand. A letter dated 2 March 1918 to Colonel Davidson from the Town Clerk of Liverpool reported an interview with Caley and James, in the latter's office in Broadway, which he considered 'very satisfactory'. In the letter the Town Clerk wrote:

'On the question of the form of the lease, I told him that the Corporation would prefer to have as lesses two or three responsible gentlemen who would be expected to give Bank references as to their responsibility, and that these gentlemen might sub-let the premises to a company or syndicate as they might desire, throughout being responsible for the payment of the rent, and the due fulfilment of the covenants of the lease. No objection was made to this suggestion.'

He also recorded that he had told James that the Corporation 'would require a minimum rent of £800 for the first two years, and subsequently a minimum rent of £1,000 a year.' These figures did not of course include the grouse moors.

Throughout the summer and autumn negotiations continued, with the Caley, James, and Lowndes syndicate the leading contenders for the lease, but struggling hard to bring rents for the hotel and the moors down to the lowest possible figures. A few other tenders were received following the advertising, but do not seem to have been serious.

As well as sustaining an offensive to lower rents, the syndicate worked hard to bring down the price of all the items they would have to buy from William Hampson. Caley made it his business to spend much of August and September at the hotel, no doubt partly for the shooting as well as business. In a long letter to Colonel Davidson on 4 September Hampson gave vent to his feelings:

'Mr Caley has made himself a perfect nuisance in the hotel, he has been there weeks prying into everything and upsetting everybody. He has complained to me of various things and I was inclined to blame Mr Bennett [the manager] but find there are two sides to consider.'

Matters had still not come to a satisfactory conclusion nearly two months later. Hampson was dismayed to hear that the syndicate's latest offer to the Corporation in respect of rent was well below the original figures demanded, being only £550 for two years and £750 for the remainder of the lease. With the possibility of this offer being refused, with all its consequences for him personally, he wrote again to Colonel Davidson on 25 October 1918, urging him to accept this offer even if it was less than the Corporation's original demand. Appalled by the thought that the syndicate might be turned down, leaving him unable to recover much of his own investment in the business, he explained that the new offer was in truth quite reasonable in view of the difficulty in finding tenants 'with sufficient capital who would be content to live in such an isolated place'. He finished his letter by saying: 'I cannot help thinking it will pay the Corporation to secure the Caley syndicate if possible, for another tenant at all suitable may take a long time to find'.

No doubt to Hampson's relief the long drawn-out proceedings were at last concluded, and the trio took up the lease in the spring of 1919, allowing him reasonable terms for the goodwill, and for the tenant's fixtures and fittings. Even though the new lessees had negotiated what they no doubt considered were the best possible terms for gaining control of the hotel and all its facilities, they were to find it as difficult as their predecessors to make a profit out of it. Some indication as to why comes from these notes written by George Westropp, who is a great-nephew of Major Lowndes:

'Major Lowndes had a joint reputation for eccentricity and generosity in our family. This combination and a background as a senior policeman in India rather than businessman goes some way towards explaining his lack of success as a hotelier.

My father recalled being collected with his mother in a pony and trap at Llanfyllin railway station and being driven the nine miles up to the lake in the summer of 1923. His uncle, Johnnie Lowndes, greeted them at the hotel and made the introductions to all the other guests over dinner. The whole hotel was filled with immediate family, other free-loading relatives and friends of the syndicate. There was not a paying guest in the house and father remembered his two week stay as a glorious house party.

Lowndes' passions were shooting and hunting. He considered trout thoroughly second rate compared with salmon fishing. Trolling a minnow was almost encouraged and Lowndes allowed his family to do so all over the lake, although the rule was only between tower and dam.

There were trips over Bwlch-y-Groes to look at a partridge shoot that the syndicate had hired in the deep valley of Llanymawddwy and much time at the kennels of Johnnie's Lake Vyrnwy Foxhounds. Anybody who knows the area or anything about hunting will tell you that Vyrnwy is not the place to hunt foxes on horseback. But, Lowndes did so and financed the whole enterprise out of the syndicate's dwindling coffers.

Those few guests who did pay, experienced an unusual diet. Johnnie had read in *The Times* that kippers were good for the brain and full of protein. He immediately sent away for a barrel of them. For a week after, there were kippers for breakfast, lunch, tea, and dinner until the residents mutinied. It did them no good. Kippers stayed on the menu until the barrel was empty. One wonders how many returned to the hotel, because regular clientele were the bread and butter of Vyrnwy as a business.

While young, I discovered a number of staff who had worked for the Major and everybody enthused over his kindness and generosity. Sick children from the village, I learned, had been sent all the way to specialists in London for treatment out of his own pocket. And 'Mervyn Davies the Tower' still takes care of a fine clock presented by Johnnie to the British Legion.

As a very small boy, I was taken to see Johnnie in an old people's nursing home near Simonsbath, Exmoor by my uncle Colonel Monty Westropp and my father. I recognised that he was rather odd. "Poor Johnnie", my father explained, "kindest man I ever met but, quite, quite hopeless with money"'

By 1925 the syndicate decided that it was time to give up the pleasant but costly trade of hotel keeping, and the lease was assigned to the Walkers, a young, recently retired Lieutenant RN and his wife Belinda. On taking over in 1926 they negotiated a new 21 year lease, due to expire in 1947. Baldwin Walker was the son of a retired Rear-Admiral, also a baronet, who was commissioner, or land agent, to the Duke of Northumberland. Belinda had been a Barnett, one of a well known Northumberland family, before her first marriage to a naval officer called Ball. It was involvement in her divorce from Ball that caused Baldwin Walker to resign from the Royal Navy, since in those days even the remotest connection with a divorce case was social and professional death in service circles.

Before coming to Lake Vyrnwy the Walkers had lived in the village of Cleobury Mortimer in Shropshire. With them came a young man called Billy Thomas, whose father owned a shop in the village, and a farm worker's daughter named Alice Turner. Both remained involved in the hotel for many years. Billy married Ida Hill, and their son John, born in 1930, also worked in it for a long time before taking on the shop at Dafarn Newydd. Alice married Walter Carpenter, member of a local family, and had a large family. She was still doing part-time work in the hotel over 50 years after coming to the valley.

Sadly Baldwin Walker contracted tuberculosis soon after arriving at Vyrnwy, and died in 1927. He was reported to have been one of the few people ever able to keep his wife under control. After his death Belinda took full charge of the hotel, and ran it with considerable flair and success. Being a strong character, without too much sympathy for other people's feelings, she rarely failed to get her own way in any business she undertook. Although not particularly good looking, and careless of her appearance, she was a vibrant personality, capable of being charming and kind as well as hard and demanding. A man to find her highly attractive was a serving Squadron-Leader, later Wing-Commander, in the RAF called Graham Martin, who began to court her soon after Walker's death. He pressed his suit by often flying over the hotel, and once or twice dropping letters for her from the air. In due course they were married, and had one son. This brought Belinda's total of children to four, since she already had a daughter by Ball, and two sons by Walker. To add to the family there was Martin's son by his first wife, named John.

John Martin, now a Lieutenant Colonel, retired from long service with the 10th Gurkha Rifles, has vivid memories of Lake Vyrnwy in the 1930s. The first was not a happy one. Aged four, he had his first meeting with his new stepmother. When she announced that she was now his mummy, was to be called mummy, and that he was to forget his other mummy and never talk about her again, he remembers running from the room shouting 'I hate you! I hate you!' This was probably in his favour in the long run, since he recalls that she treated people better who stood up to her. Those who did not could be trampled upon if necessary.

His father was a charming, easy-going Irishman with an altogether different character. He loved flying, motor-racing, shooting, and fishing and had little aptitude for business. To his son he was not only a kind father but a good friend, who took a delight in passing on his own knowledge of field sports. On 20 September 1937 Graham's game-book proudly records: 'Took John out with his gun for the first time.' The two of them shot a brace of grouse, a duck, and a rabbit on this occasion.

Before the Second World War most guests changed into dinner jackets and long evening dresses for dinner. Those who did not could be made to feel uncomfortable. A permanent resident in the hotel for some years was Lieutenant-Colonel the Hon Robert Lygon, late of the Grenadier Guards, whose beady eye was quickly turned on anyone he considered unsuitably dressed.

Perhaps young John Martin's happiest times were spent with members of the staff. John Hill taught him how to look after a pony, and how to clean his tack properly, as well as passing on much country lore. Mrs Hill, who was always dressed in Victorian style with a cameo brooch at the throat of her high black collar, was unfailingly kind to him when he visited her house. He remembers all the other members of the family with great affection as well. Another good friend was Billy Thomas, with whom he often travelled in one of the two cars kept at the hotel, the Rolls-Royce pictured in one of the illustrations, or the big, wooden-bodied, Ford shooting-brake. Among the indoor staff Mary Morris, the chambermaid, was a great favourite.

Another person to remember well the 1930s is Mrs Doris Moss, in those days Miss Grey, usually known as Dolly, who worked in the hotel as secretary and receptionist. She has recorded some interesting recollections of the times:

'When I first arrived at Lake Vyrnwy, the hotel was very different structurally. The present pantry was the housekeeper's room, 'the piggery', where the housekeeper, the receptionist and the 'chicken lady' ate and sat, sometimes being invaded by family and regular visitors at busy times. The refrigerator was downstairs, one very large one with different compartments for freshwater fish, sea fish, meat etc. at different temperatures. The present dining room was divided, there being the steward's room at one end and the part nearest the office was the bar. The present bar was the large dining-room and the present drawing room was the small dining-room. The drawing room was on the first floor where No. 1 now is.

The kitchen had an old-fashioned coal fired range and there was an old-fashioned bread oven in the back yard where part of The Tavern now is. The kitchen boy had to collect wood and light the fire in the oven as required. We baked all our own bread.

We were very much more self-supporting. We had our own cows and only had to buy milk and cream when the hotel was full. We also had our own sheep and our own free range chickens. Eggs had to be bought in the high season only. We also put down eggs during the winter for use for cooking in the summer. We also killed our own fowl. We usually had sex-linked cockerels for table birds. We had sows and a boar. The piglets were sold about six weeks old. This was an amusing business as Stanley Davies from Llanfyllin, a brother of the late Rt Hon Clement Davies, M.P, would come and bargain with John Hill our farm bailiff and then come to the office where the deal was made and Stanley Davies departed with the piglets – and a bottle of whisky.

Dry goods came once a month from Hudson Bros., London, meat from Brodricks, Liverpool, but home killed meat from Embrey at Nesscliffe. Butter came from Wathes Bros, a Shropshire firm. Mac-Fisheries supplied a certain amount of fish. Their representative called one day during the summer to offer us frozen pheasants – quite regardless of the fact that we sold them fresh pheasants after every syndicate shoot.

One year we had let a certain part of the pheasant shoot to two old gentlemen and they had come up in August to see how the birds were coming on. One evening at dinner time a guest came to inform us that his son had gone out rabbit shooting, without permission, and had not returned. A search party was just being organised when he returned carrying two pheasant chicks he had shot on the rearing field. Naturally, the two old gentlemen saw the boy arrive and things became awkward. Eventually one of the old gentlemen demanded compensation from the boy's father and when it was forthcoming the other gentlemen insisted it should be given to the church offertory. The guest and his son left the next day.

In August there was usually an evening picnic at the top end of the lake for the younger and more adventurous guests, who would sometimes help to remove the chub from the shallow water by various means – kicking, spearing, shooting or tickling. Those picnics were quite a hazard and it seemed that every fly, midge and mosquito in the neighbourhood joined in, and even a smudge fire did not improve the situation.

There were also Treasure Hunts and also occasionally on moonlight nights drives round the lake in open cars shooting at rabbits – the gun sitting on the bonnet.

During the summer evening dress was worn every night except Sunday and there was often dancing to gramophone records after dinner.

At the beginning of July each year Liverpool Corporation members descended in strength. The Lord Mayor had his footmen in attendance and he wore his Mayoral Chain for their special dinner. They had the small dining room (as it then was) at their disposal and the upstairs drawing-room as a sitting room. On one occasion they had just left after tea in the drawing-room when one or two regular visitors wanted tea, so it was suggested they should go up to the drawing-room to get away from the crowd. About ten minutes later a rather shaken guest came down to say that part of the ceiling had fallen on them.

This also happened once in the present bar on Good Friday morning. A very upset barman came to the office saying that a large lump of ceiling just by the fireplace had fallen missing him by inches. Humphrey Howard came to the rescue.

Every year in September there was the Sheep Sale. Liverpool Corporation sold a large number of sheep and we sold some of ours. The sale was held in the field above the hotel and meals were served in the staff room, steward's room, and the dining room most of the day. Guests were warned about this but many enjoyed the whole show. The numbers of sellers, shepherds etc. that came for a meal, to be put down to Mr Stanley Davies account, was quite surprising, but the account was never queried.

In the winter of 1937 we had the experience of being snowed up. We were lucky that it happened on a Saturday night, when we had about a dozen guests in the hotel, as we had collected our stores and fresh vegetables on Friday. The snow started about 10 p.m. and there was about an inch of snow by 11.00 p.m. During the night the wind rose and there was quite a blizzard. The snow was up to the glass on the front door by morning and many trees were down all round the lake and also patches of several hundred had been toppled. The telephone wires were down and the roads were blocked.

The visitors and staff passed the time in the afternoons tobogganing down from the front drive over the field to the road on old tea trays. It was several days before the roads were cleared for traffic to get through with supplies and the village was getting short of bread and flour.

One year the British Waterways Association decided to have their Annual General Meeting at Lake Vyrnwy, which involved our having to supply lunch and tea for 350. It was decided that a marquee would be put up on the tennis court. As far as I remember they had hot soup but otherwise it was a cold meal. We had to hire waitresses and a certain amount of crockery but we decided to order 400 new coffee cups from Wedgwood & Co, Stoke-on-Trent. These went missing on the railway and arrived the evening before the great day. As you can imagine the telephone lines were red hot.

For some time we used to do meals for coach parties which had to be booked in advance. It could be frustrating as whatever menus were suggested they always wanted tomato soup and roast chicken.

On one occasion a high tea had been arranged for a party walking over from Arran Mawddwy to arrive about 5.00 p.m. It was nearly seven o'clock when the phone rang and we were informed they had lost one of the party but most of them would be arriving. This turned out to be a tragedy as one boy had strayed and had fallen over a ledge and had been killed. The press got hold of the story and the telephone rang incessantly. We eventually persuaded everyone that they would get more information from Dinas Mawddwy as the search party had set out from there. In the end we rang the exchange and said we would not accept any more calls until the morning.

As explained in an earlier chapter, the Humphrey Howard mentioned by Doris Moss as 'coming to the rescue' was the Corporation's resident agent on the estate. Belinda took care to maintain an excellent rapport with Humphrey, and he came to her rescue on many occasions.

Although the storm-clouds were gathering over Europe during the second half of the 1930s, and thoughtful people were increasingly worried about the resurgence of a belligerent Germany ruled by Adolf Hitler, life was pleasant for such people as had the wherewithal to stay at Lake Vyrnwy. Under Belinda's efficient management the hotel was well run and adequately prosperous, while Graham Martin's knowledge of field sports ensured that the sporting side flourished, as can be seen in the chapters devoted to that aspect.

For a short period after the declaration of war with Germany on 3 September 1939 there was little change in the way of life in rural areas like the Vyrnwy valley. The pinch was first felt when men started to be called away to serve in the armed forces, or to do some form of civilian work devoted to the war effort. Graham Martin was soon back in RAF uniform, while Billy Thomas was in due course directed to factory work near Wolverhampton. Many Corporation workers were similarly called up, with only a proportion given reserved occupation status in order to keep the estate going. Those that remained at home were employed in forestry and farming: there was no labour available for luxuries like shooting and fishing. Only a few elderly men past retirement age were available to act as occasional boatmen on the lake, while the switch of all the game-keepers to other work meant that only rough shooting could take place. In spite of many difficulties the hotel itself flourished during the war, as will unfold in the following chapter.

# CHAPTER FIVE

## The Second Half Century, 1940–1992

In direct contrast to William Hampson's experience during the First World War, the Second was for Belinda Martin the busiest and most profitable period in her long tenancy of the hotel. For some five years hardly a night passed without every bed in the place full, sometimes using unusual rooms to provide extra accommodation. On a visit to the hotel in the 1970s the elderly Belinda was walking along the first floor corridor when she passed the door of the ladies lavatory, at the time situated near the top of the back stairs. 'Often shoved a couple of extra beds in there in the war,' she announced. During the war the vicar moved out of the large, stone-built vicarage which then stood on the site of the present much smaller house; it was later pulled down because of dry rot. Quick to spot an opportunity, Belinda contrived to obtain use of it as an annexe to the hotel. A remarkable range of people occupied the hotel in the war years. A royal family must head the list. After the occupation of their country by the Japanese in 1942 King Prajadhipok of Siam with his Queen, and the Crown Prince with his wife and baby, were given refuge in Britain. To provide them with a safe place to stay Lake Vyrnwy was chosen, and they made the hotel their home for over two years. They occupied five of the best rooms on the first floor overlooking the lake, and were looked after devotedly by Ida Thomas and her sister Gwen, who remember them with great affection.

Under a scheme instigated by Lord Nuffield, the car manufacturer, and bearing his name, Lake Vyrnwy became an official leave centre for officers of the armed forces. Among the many who took advantage of the scheme the majority were airmen, including a high proportion of Polish pilots. A number of Dutch officers from the Netherlands army contingent based around Wolverhampton also frequented the hotel. Belinda enjoyed the company of the Poles, reputedly to an unusual extent in one or two cases, but that may have been just gossip. Other servicemen to come on leave included those who did so under their own private arrangements, using petrol coupons which were allowed in small quantities for this purpose. Among this group were Wing Commander James Moir, AFC, with his wife Ruth and two sons, who always endeavoured to spend his occasional spells of leave at Vyrnwy.

There were even a few officers to be found in the hotel towards the end of the war who were in the area on duty. After the successful breaching of the Mohne dam in Germany by the 'Dambusters' in 1943, it was feared that the Luftwaffe might attempt a retaliatory attack on some major dam in Britain. A troop of anti-aircraft guns was therefore sent to Vyrnwy, and took up positions to protect the dam. The officers were accommodated in the hotel, while the soldiers used a large hut erected near the estate offices at the south end of the dam. This hut was dismantled after the war and re-erected opposite the side-door of the hotel on the site of the erstwhile post office. Here it was used for many years as a games-room and store, or as a rod room.

The list of war time occupants is by no means finished. The next group to be mentioned was composed of the masters and boys of a small preparatory school, evacuated from a dangerous home in the south of England. A large number of rooms on the top floor of the hotel were allotted to the school, as well as the bungalow in the grounds, now known as 'The Cottage', as already explained.

Even with all these varieties of people staying in the hotel there was always room for ordinary civilian visitors to be squeezed in wherever possible. In addition, members of the Liverpool City Council, and officials of the Corporation, continued to make their regular visits: indeed there was every temptation to do so whenever possible, since peaceful nights and access to farm produce were preferable to bombs on the city and rationing.

The negligible risk of bombing, added to the presence of a lot of young officers enjoying a spell of rest and tranquillity, produced a happy atmosphere in the hotel. Such discomforts as there were could easily be ignored by people inured to far worse conditions elsewhere in war-time Britain, or overseas in theatres of action. Most evenings there was dancing in the hall to a radiogram. Ruth Moir remembers periods of leave during the war as particularly enjoyable, though there was one aspect which she and Jamie found an embarrassment.

Strict food, rationing made hotel catering difficult for everyone, especially in the towns. In rural areas like Montgomeryshire it was made easier by access to such treasures as eggs, butter, and bacon purchased from farms, which in those days almost invariably provided such items for themselves. Billy Thomas was often on the road to farms all over the countryside to pick up quantities of these treasured goods. The trouble was that the distribution of them to the hotel residents was not entirely fair. Belinda organised the dining-room in such a way that she sat at a large table for up to 16 people, situated in the far side of the central pillar which still divides the room more or less into two parts. At this table sat her favoured young airmen, and special friends such as the Moirs, who had known the Martins for many years, going back to the time when Jamie and Graham had served in the same squadron in the RAF in the early 1930s. While the guests in the large end of the dining-room made do with largely rationed food, the quality of that served at Belinda's private table was almost up to pre-war standards. Knowing what was being doled out to most of their fellow guests made the Moirs feel awkward about eating their own sumptuous meals.

To keep the hotel running satisfactorily a supply of petrol was essential, not only for Billy's foraging expeditions to farms, but for meeting guests from, and delivering them to, various railway stations and picking-up points. To obtain the necessary quantities of strictly rationed fuel Belinda used all her wiles and guile, playing the importance of the leave centre as her trump card in her legal search for extra petrol coupons. Having little time for regulations or red tape, she was not averse to picking them up in the black market as well. Using every possible means she managed to keep the wheels of the hotel vehicles rolling throughout the war.

The vehicle most used was the Ford V8 shooting-brake,

with its body-work made of wood, as was the fashion in those days. There were two main collecting-cum-delivery points for guests: Llanfyllin railway station, and a halt two miles east on the line to Oswestry. This, however, was not used for meeting trains, but as a point to collect people coming from Oswestry by taxi. Its significance lay in the fact that it was just ten miles from the town, and therefore on the extreme limit of the distance which war-time regulations allowed a taxi to travel on any one journey. (Bryngwyn halt, as it was called, was demolished when the railway line to Llanfyllin was closed in the 1960s.)

As the war neared its close in 1945 a small incident occurred which was to have quite an effect on the future of the hotel. The Lord Mayor of Liverpool and one of his senior colleagues came to Vyrnwy for an important meeting with Humphrey Howard. They were not given good rooms, but put into two singles on the first floor at the back, directly over the hall, where next morning at 2 a.m a cheerful, noisy party was still in progress. The Lord Mayor could not get to sleep. Accompanied by his colleague, both in pyjamas and dressing gowns, he appeared on the stairs and ordered the party to be brought to an end, and the noisy members of it, mainly airmen, to go to bed. 'Don't you know there's a war on,' shouted one very large young pilot, who promptly ran up the stairs and picked the Lord Mayor up bodily. Others dealt similarly with his partner, and the two protesting dignitaries were carried to their rooms, told to shut up, and dumped on their beds. The party was then resumed. Had Belinda been present she would undoubtedly have stopped the proceedings at an early stage: though prepared to treat the Lord Mayor in a fairly casual fashion, she would have realised that this was going a little too far.

In May 1945 VE day was celebrated with the relief and abandon seen in the rejoicing all over Britain. When VJ day came in August, Ruth Moir happened to be staying in the hotel with her two sons. On hearing of the Japanese surrender, Belinda at once announced that everyone due to leave that day must stay for a party that night. When it was pointed out that nearly all the guests she referred to were about to depart, with a whole mass of new ones coming in to take their places, she remained unmoved. Declaring that this was of no importance, she ordered mattresses to be put on the floors of all the larger rooms, and announced that everyone could double up for such hours of the night that would remain after the party. Ruth and her two sons found themselves in room 39 as three out of a total of eight occupants. But nobody minded, or if they did they knew it was no use complaining.

About this time Belinda remembered that her 21 year lease was due to end in the spring of 1947. Assuming that there would be no difficulty in renewing it, she applied to the Corporation to do so, but to her amazement, and fury, her application was refused. Undoubtedly the recent treatment of the Lord Mayor had done little to help her cause. It is likely that various officials from Liverpool had received more cavalier treatment than they felt their position deserved during war-time visits, even if not quite so extreme as that meted out to the Lord Mayor. All this had built up a determination at city headquarters to find a new tenant for the hotel, and this was a problem for Belinda which Humphrey Howard was not able to solve for her.

In 1946 Jamie Moir ended his service in the RAF, and determined to take up farming. Having been brought up and worked on his father's large farm in New Zealand, before coming to Britain to join the RAF in the 1920s, he had a good knowledge of farming practice, especially with livestock. As they had grown very fond of the Vyrnwy area during many visits to the hotel, he and Ruth came to stay there, as a base from which to start searching for a farm in the neighbourhood. On discovering that Belinda's application for renewal had been turned down, and that tenders were being sought from new potential tenants, they decided to make an offer themselves. The 435-acre hotel farm would give Jamie his chance to indulge in his interest in that direction, while Ruth found the prospect of helping to run the hotel more attractive than that of being purely a farmer's wife.

14 November 1946 was the closing date for tenders, and five days later the Town Clerk listed the particulars of six people who had put in serious offers. Of these, the Moirs and three others were asked to come to Liverpool on 25 November to be interviewed by the Water Committee, who decided

that of the four they were the ones to be granted the lease, even though their offer was not the highest.

Having successfully achieved their aim of becoming lessees, the Moirs soon discovered that their troubles were only just beginning. When she learnt that she was to lose her lease Belinda lost interest in the business. She spent several months of 1946 touring Africa with some of her Polish friends, leaving Graham Martin to supervise the hotel in a rather luke-warm fashion. Following the hectic years of the war, when little maintenance could be carried out, this period of inattention by the proprietors saw the condition of the hotel, the farm, and the grounds sink into a state of general dilapidation. To compound the difficulty of coming to terms with Belinda in respect of a realistic figure to be paid for the contents of the hotel, the goodwill, and the other assets of the business, the early months of 1947, while all this was being sorted out, saw the longest and coldest winter of the century enfold the country in a deep blanket of snow and ice. For some weeks no motor vehicles could get through to the valley, and supplies for Llanwddyn and the hotel came on horse drawn sledges, or in panniers on the back of a horse. Any person needing to travel to or from the area had to walk much of the way to Llanfyllin along a narrow track between high banks of snow.

Eventually more or less satisfactory terms were arranged with Belinda, who is remembered departing from the hotel on a horse-drawn sledge, accompanied by the man from Jackson Stopps and Staff, who had been sent to value the stock and contents, perched on the back, looking thoroughly incongruous in a bowler hat. The Moirs moved in just as the thaw began in early April, to spend their first night in the hotel in a leaking bed-room, where they were forced to move buckets around at frequent intervals to catch drops from the ceiling. Because of the appalling state of the building, made worse by the ravages of the winter, the Corporation eventually agreed to spend over £2,000 – a big sum then – in redecorating it and repairing the roof. The decision to do this, and so give the Moirs a reasonable start, was largely due to the intercession of Humphrey Howard, who was to prove himself as good an ally to them as he had been to their predecessors.

A great strength of Lake Vyrnwy Hotel has always been the loyalty and efficiency of its long serving staff. The Moirs were fortunate to take on many key employees who had spent most of their lives working there. Having known the hotel well as guests, they had the advantage of knowing the majority of their new staff quite well already. Members of the Hill family and their dependants were strongly represented. John, son of Billy and Ida Thomas, had joined his parents in the hotel, and in 1949 was put in charge of the tap-room at the young age of 19. He was to fill this position with great efficiency for the next 25 years. Another family with several members involved were the Morris's. Mary and her niece Annie were chambermaids, and Mary's brother Joey was a regular boatman. Another chambermaid, Milly Barrett, is still working in the hotel at the time of writing, giving evidence of the remarkable loyalty and vigour of the long serving staff.

The weak link in the employment chain was in the kitchen. The practice was to hire chefs for 'the season', which meant the period from Easter each year to November. In 1947 a pleasant Swiss man was taken on, but proved an indifferent cook. He returned in 1948, but the food he produced was so bad that Ruth Moir suggested he should be removed. Instead, she promoted an Italian prisoner-of-war, who had been employed as a kitchen porter, to take his place. Under her supervision Vittorio Cottiga, who had a natural flair for cooking, blossomed into an excellent chef. When he eventually left, Ruth, who had done some courses at the Cordon Bleu school, took charge of the kitchen herself. Over the years a stream of girls came to help her and learn from her. These were mainly daughters and relations of the Moirs' personal friends, or of regular hotel guests. The style of cooking she developed was based on relatively simple, even homely, recipes, but adjusted for large numbers. Excellent soups, including proper home made consommé, pâtés, game, roasts, and simple puddings were the mainstay of menus which were greatly appreciated by the type of guests who enjoyed similar food in their own homes. Those who were out each day on the lake fishing, or some other activity, particularly appreciated the generous breakfasts and substantial packed lunches.

On taking over the hotel farm Jamie Moir was faced with the prospect of a difficult period of reorganisation before it could run again to his satisfaction. During the war fences and gates had fallen into sad disrepair, and required a great deal of work to put right. Fortunately the Corporation helped with this to some extent. The terrible winter of 1947 had wreaked havoc among the sheep flocks in the district, with the carcases of dead sheep lying everywhere as the snows finally melted. Such animals as were left alive were in a poor state, while the lambs born to the few ewes which survived were weak and sickly, an easy prey to the numerous and hungry foxes which proliferated at the time. Eventually the hotel flock was built up again to a strength of 400 breeding ewes, whose lambs were the most sought after of all those sold each September at the sales held in the field to the north of the hotel, at the top of the rise beyond The Tavern.

The hotel farm's 435 acres were divided into two parts: 89 acres of low-ground land, and 346 acres of sheep-walk. For a few years some oats were grown each summer on the low-ground. In the autumn a threshing machine would trundle up to the hotel to be set up at the end of the farm buildings below the doors of what was then the granary. The threshed corn was kept for feeding stock, and the straw stacked to be cut up as chaff for the same purpose in the winter.

As the years passed the labour force on the farm was reduced by economic pressure. The first to go was Sammy Hill, who had followed his father John as bailiff. By the end of the 1950s Jamie was working the farm almost single handed, with only occasional help, as well as running the hotel. Even his remarkable constitution could not stand the pace for ever, and when his back started to give him trouble he was forced to give up the tenancy of most of the land in 1961. However, he retained some fifteen acres close to the hotel on which to keep two or three Jersey cows to provide milk for the hotel. These he milked himself every day, thus keeping some contact with the farming which was his first love.

During the Moirs' years the hotel was run with meticulous

efficiency, and kept spotlessly clean throughout. The polished furniture in the public rooms and the top of the resident's bar always gleamed. The relatively formal way in which the daily routine was conducted suited most of the guests, many of whom had service backgrounds like the proprietors themselves. They expected to have dinner at a set time, and to dress tidily for it. Such people as did not enjoy the atmosphere did not stay long, often having been made aware that they were not particularly welcome. For the important regular guests nothing was ever too much trouble, and many of them came once or twice a year for quite long stays.

As the year 1968 approached, so did the end of the 21 year lease granted to the Moirs in 1947. They decided to apply for an extension of five years, to run from 1968 to 1973. The Liverpool Corporation was quite agreeable to this, but wished to decide on a new rent at the start of the extended period. They commissioned Harper, Webb and Co, a Chester firm of chartered surveyors, to inspect the hotel and make a recommendation as to what the annual rent should be. Two paragraphs from their report give a good insight into the Moirs' guardianship of the hotel:

'Although Mr Moir had apparently no experience of the hotel trade prior to his taking occupation of the Lake Vyrnwy Hotel in 1947, from our comparatively brief association with him on the occasion of our inspection of the property we formed the opinion that he has natural aptitude as a proprietor and we were very favourably impressed by what we saw of the manner in which the establishment is being run. Due to the great difficulty in obtaining regular staff both he and his wife are, we understand, regularly engaged in providing services well beyond the scope of what we would expect from the proprietors of a hotel of this size, such as cultivation and maintenance of the gardens and grounds and all of the cooking. There is no doubt that they display great industry and resource in not only running the business but also maintaining the property in a manner that exceeds their strict obligations under the lease . . .

In the circumstances we find it difficult to quote a hard

and fast figure as our opinion of the rental value of this property in the open market on the terms quoted to us, on which an extension of the present lease would be granted for a further five years. In fact, on the basis of the figures shown in the accounts, we examined, we think that the Corporation would be hard put to find another tenant able and willing to carry on the established business in place of the present lessee who, so he informs us, is able to supplement his return by a private income.'

Based on the Harper Webb recommendations the rent offered by the Moirs' was accepted, and their lease was renewed for five years. As the 1960s ended age began to take it toll of some long serving members of the staff. Due to heart trouble Billy Thomas was forced to work for only a few hours a day, with a fraction of his former energy. Selwyn Jones was recruited to help him, and gradually took over the job of hotel porter from him: a job he is still doing over 20 years later. Mary Morris retired from being a full-time chamber-maid, though she was allowed to keep a room in the hotel, and lived there until her death at the age of 80. She had worked in it all her life, from the age of 15, when she started as the staff maid. A year or two later Ida Thomas also retired, after over 50 years of good service. Not only were members of the staff feeling the weight of the passing years, but even Jamie Moir's stammina was being taxed as he approached his 70th birthday, leading him to make the decision to retire in 1972.

From here on the story must be told in the first person. While Jamie was anxious to retire, Ruth, some 14 years his junior, wished to carry on with the business. To do so she needed a partner, to look after the numerous jobs which had been her husband's responsibility, and in particular to run the sporting estate. One attempt to set up such a partnership had fallen through shortly before I came to stay at Vyrnwy in May 1972, having finished 26 years in the regular army the previous month. I was combining a stay at the hotel, with my wife and my father, with a visit to a firm in Birmingham where I had been offered the possibility of a job. Arriving at the head office of the firm I found that the job had been provisionally offered to someone else already. However, knowing of Ruth's search for a partner I wondered whether to suggest myself as a candidate. After a day of fishing and discussion on the lake with my wife and father I decided to do so. My offer was accepted; a partnership agreement was drawn up; a new 21 year lease was negotiated; and on 1 November 1972 Ruth and I started in business together.

Apart from one or two bumps in the early years, the course of our partnership ran remarkably smoothly. This was mainly due to a clear definition of responsibilities between us, and an avoidance on both sides of interference in the other's domain. Even if, looking back over the 14 plus years we worked together, there were things I now think we could have done better, I am grateful that such harmony prevailed between us. I gather that small business partnerships are not often so successful in this direction, and I must pay full tribute to Ruth for being such a splendid colleague to work with, who so consistently maintained the highest standards in her department.

I am not going to say much more about the years 1972 to 1986 before recounting the story of our purchase of the freehold of the hotel, and the sale of the new owner. In other chapters there is mention of the improvements we made to the buildings, and of the build-up of the pheasant shoot. However, I would like to quote extracts from two books which gave us pleasure in our last full year in business together. *The Good Food Guide* in 1986 made these comments:

> 'There are few concessions to modernity at Mrs Moir's shooting-lodge above the lake, which she has run since 1947. Good-value menus include home-made soups, mixed fish quiche, cold meats, traditional roasts, salads, marvellous chutneys and good old-style bread-and-butter pudding. Coffee is served in the sumptuous lounge. Game is shot on the estate. . . . The non-vintage and inexpensive wine list includes a few bargains, such as St Julien '80, from the Barton stable, at £7.50.'

Somewhat to our surprise, but definitely to our delight. *The Good Hotel Guide* gave us one of its ten *César Awards* for

1986. These awards, it explains, 'are given for different sorts of excellence among hotels in Britain and Ireland.' Our citation read as follows:

> 'For preserving traditional values in a sporting hotel. Colonel Sir John Baynes and Mrs Moir know what they are about. They make no concessions to any modern image, but maintain with conspicuous success the virtues of a comfortable old-fashioned sporting hotel.'

When the Lake Vyrnwy estate was about to be passed from the Liverpool Corporation to the Severn-Trent Water Authority in 1973, I had written to the Corporation offering to purchase the freehold of the hotel and the sporting rights. This followed an unofficial enquiry among the tenants as to which of them might be interested in buying their freeholds. In the end the decision was made at headquarters in Liverpool that no sales would be made, and when the S-TWA assumed control on 1 April 1974 it decided to carry on the Corporation policy of retaining all property on the watershed of the lake in its own hands.

Then, in 1984, we suddenly heard that the S-TWA might be changing its mind on the subject, and that the offers of tenants to buy their freeholds might be given consideration. Ruth and I decided to test the matter out, and wrote to say that we wished to buy the hotel and its 36 acres of grounds. Receiving a positive response, we set about negotiating terms and conditions of purchase, and in 1985 became the freeholders of the property. Early the following year we came to a decision to end our partnership, as both of us wanted to climb off what might be called the 'tread-mill' of hotel-keeping to pursue other interests.

The sale of the hotel was put in the hands of Robert Barry and Co of Cirencester. The partner in charge of negotiations was Mr Hugh Guillebaud. During the summer of 1986 some thirty potential buyers came to look over the hotel and the grounds. When tenders were called for in September there were nine serious offers. Of these, that of Mr Jim Bisiker was accepted. It was arranged that the actual hand-over of the hotel to his general manager, Mr Jim Talbot, would take

1 The Vyrnwy valley during the building of the dam. The start of the road over the dam from the north side is in the immediate foreground. In the distance can be seen the foundations of the straining tower, and beyond that the old village of Llanwddyn

2  The hotel in about 1893

**LAKE VYRNWY HOTEL.**      **N. WALES, VIA OSWESTRY.**
Station, Llanfyllin, Cambrian Railway. LAKE VYRNWY covers 1,100 acres; 650 reserved for fly only. The Loch Leven
trout only.     Apply, MISS DAVIES, as above.

4   A party of four guns and their ladies on the moor in about 1900. It appears to have been a walking-up day. At the back is head-keeper, Tom Hughes, with two assistant keepers

5  Major Lowndes with his hounds, and Miss Ruby Hill, his whipper-in, in the field above the hotel in April 1923

6  An aerial view of the hotel taken by Squadron-Leader Graham Martin on 26 March 1928, at the time he was courting his future wife, Belinda

7  Beaters on the moors in the late 1920s. On the left Joe Morris with the pony. The tall man next to him is Trevor Hill. Then Walter Carpenter with hands in his breeches' pockets, and Tom Hughes standing in a rain-coat

8   Guests and boatmen after the annual Boatmen's Fishing Competition in the late 1930 – taken outside the main entrance of the Hotel. *Back Row:* Mr Jack Roberts, A. N. Other, Mr Larman, Mr King, Captain Tanner, Mr Humphrey Howard, Mrs M. Martin, Commander Taylor and Mr Graham Martin. *Middle Row:* Mr Cadwallader Williams, Edwin Humphries, 'Sim' Carpenter, Walter Carpenter, Albert Carpenter and George Morris. *Front Row:* 'Willy' Edwards, Felix Evans, Bernard Hughes, Owen Thomas, 'Willy' Morris, 'Sim' Carpenter Jnr, 'Joey' Morris, Harry Jones, Joe Morris and Bob Roberts

place on 1 February 1987. All members of the staff were told that they would be taken on by the new owners from that date if they wished to continue working for them. During the final week-end of the old regime Iain Gregory, who had run the residents' bar with great efficiency since 1980, unfortunately suffered a collapsed lung and had to be rushed into hospital. Due to his ill-health he and his wife Jeannie, who had been such an excellent secretary and receptionist in the hotel during the same period, were the only members of the staff unable to carry on under the new management.

As explained in the acknowledgements section at the beginning of the book, Mr Jim Bisiker formed the company called Market Glen to run the business for him. I remained in partnership with the company with the primary task of showing Brian Bisiker, who was given charge of the sporting side, all that I could about this vital aspect of the hotel's affairs. Under the guidance of Jim Talbot, who was appointed managing director of Market Glen, an extensive programme of work was put in hand to restore and refurbish the ground floor rooms in the hotel, and to modernise the bed-rooms upstairs. This was a natural continuation of the process, mentioned in Chapter 3, whereby each generation has found it necessary to alter and up-date the buildings in some way. The quality of the work done has been of a very high order, and the main public-rooms have been redecorated with care to make them more comfortable without destroying their traditional charm.

Naturally enough, the prospect of change gave rise to some misgivings among the regular visitors who knew and loved the hotel in its previous state. Although there are some who have ceased to come to it, most of the old, regular guests have renewed their patronage, and still return at their accustomed times to pursue their special interests. Among these well-established supporters are some intrepid motor-cyclists, a group of whom were first brought to Vyrnwy in 1972 by Mr Peter Sheen, who is to-day Director-General of the British Motor-cycle Industry Association. Calling themselves 'The Club', these 20 or more senior executives from the motor industry should not be thought of as elderly 'Hell's Angels', but properly regarded as responsible citizens, in spite of their somewhat bizarre outfits when setting out on their motor-cycle tours of the Welsh countryside!

In 1984 the 21st Anniversary of this organisation's existence was celebrated at the hotel, and guest of honour was the famous John Surtees, renowned as having been world racing champion on both 'two and four wheels'. Due to the fact that the members enjoyed the hotel's excellent house Bordeaux, Tanner's claret, and on one occasion drank the cellar dry of it, the name of their club was eventually changed to the 'Tanner's Club'. In honour of this they were all invited to an excellent dinner in 1991 in the head office, and main cellars, of Tanners Wines in Shrewsbury. Since the hotel's wines had been provided by this remarkable private firm of wine merchants for well over half a century this was a most appropriate occasion.

As well as retaining the support of the majority of its long-standing patrons, the hotel has been successful in attracting many new visitors since it came under different management. Much credit for this must go to the marketing skills of Mrs Nikki Bisiker, who handles this aspect of the business with such flair. From the point of view of all those who have known Lake Vyrnwy over a long stretch of time, and regard it as a very special place, the way in which Jim Bisiker and those who work for him have been able to modernise the hotel, without losing its charm, is a matter for which to be profoundly grateful.

*Part III*

*The Sporting Side*

# CHAPTER SIX

# The Story of Trout Fishing on the Lake

## By G. V. Westropp

'If you can catch a trout on Lake Vyrnwy, you can catch a trout anywhere,' said 'Sim' Carpenter, that skilled Vyrnwy boatman, when he was patiently trying to teach me to cast a fly 40 years ago. I have fished on many waters at home and abroad since then and still have no argument with his sentiment.

Indeed, this magnificent lake in Mid-Wales presents the type of angling challenge that brings fishermen back time and time again.

For years, Lake Vyrnwy could claim to be the largest man-made reservoir in the British Isles. Its splendid masonry dam – Europe's biggest – Rhine-like straining tower and heavily timbered surrounding hills and crags, provide the angler with the perfect setting for his or her sport.

During the first years after 1,121 acres of the Llanwddyn Valley were finally flooded in 1889, as already mentioned, the lake produced good trout of just over 1 lb average. At odd intervals over the past 100 years – and particularly since 1980 – it has managed to repeat the performance.

Food is, of course, a vital factor in any trout fishery and that is just one of the problems for the Vyrnwy fish in their endless fight for survival.

When first flooded with 13 million gallons of water food was plentiful, as much of the valley now covered up to the present normal level of the lake was farmland.

After the first glut, the trout had a much tougher time filling their stomachs and their average size dropped as the original surface soil was washed away to leave bare rock. The dark acid peat water from the mountains destroyed nearly all vegetation and, with a few exceptions, stopped essential growth of water weed.

For the most part throughout the four-and-a-half-mile length of Vyrnwy, the shore line is now plain Cambrian rock or shale beach with the sides shelving steeply away into the water.

Vyrnwy is a long narrow lake with many bays and indentations served by torrent rivers and streamlets. There are, however, several larger bays. Rhiwargor and Eunant – the major arms that branch at the top end – Llywn Rhiw on the south bank and Cedig on the north, are the most notable.

Of these, Rhiwargor is the shallowest and is often half empty during the dry months of mid-summer. Since grass and weed tend to grow there virtually every season creating a reliable food supply, the trout are more numerous and are usually in better condition. A further favourable factor is the main feeder river which enters the lake at its head with the consequent additional supply of nourishment. Other popular fishing spots are the sizeable streams that drop into the lake at Cedig, Llywn Rhiw and Eunant.

At the dam end, the two large tunnels diverting waters from the adjoining valleys of Afon Cownwy and Afon Marchnant pour out their wealth of water and food. The fish incline to cluster around these and they are favourite spawning runs in October and November when there is enough water in the lake to allow the trout to get up.

What of the fishing itself? It can – and does – vary considerably both in location and time of the year.

Being 800 feet up in the Welsh hills, Vyrnwy can be a cold place in winter with the warmer weather of spring arriving several weeks later than the lower-lying parts of the country. The water is slow to rise in temperature with the trout just as slow to start moving. An early Easter can be a freezing experience.

May and June see an improvement in both trout activity and sport. However, a very hot spell in mid-summer can have much the same effect on the fish as the cold of early spring bringing a fatal lethargy – as far as the fly-fisherman is concerned – to the trouts' movements. The cooler weather of the last few weeks of the season will often sharpen their appetites once more.

Obviously, the fishing is better where the water provides a

fuller larder for the trout. So the places already mentioned are the more rewarding. Rhiwargor, Cedig, Llwyn Rhiw and the two tunnels are all prime examples of this but there are numerous little inlets just as satisfying to the angler. The beach affectionately known as Mrs Morris's and the Tower Beat are often excellent spots. Even the Boat House Pool has its fans – particularly when the lake is too rough for either comfort or safety.

Lake Vyrnwy is in so many respects far closer in character to a natural mountain lake, i.e. the lochs of the Scottish Highlands, than the other man-made reservoirs like Rutland, Grafham, Chew and Bewl Bridge. These look and fish as differently from Vyrnwy as chalk from cheese.

Even the brown trout themselves behave and fight differently from their lowland brothers. For one thing, a high proportion of Vyrnwy 'brownies' are home grown – 'natives' – having started their lives in the gravel of the many feeder streams. Nearly all the lowland reservoir fish come from trout farms.

Stocking Vyrnwy would seem unnecessary due to the multiplicity of spawning streams. This is not the case. The lake has to be stocked to some extent to maintain a 'head' of reasonably sized fish.

Apart from those caught during the season it is estimated that as few as a third of the thousands of fish that run up the two tunnels and other main feeders each autumn return the following spring. The reasons appear to be a combination of predators, both human and animal, and sheer exhaustion. So stocking goes on.

The practice of stocking fish into the lake started in the early years but in earnest from 1929. It has been an annual event ever since, with the exception of the Second World War years. Recently an average of over 2,000 brown trout and rainbows have been entered – spread between the end of February and May. Stock fish have come from the Chirk Fishery Company throughout all these years.

At odd times, good sized rainbows – up to 3 lb – have been put in with some spectacular results. Since the rainbow is a migratory fish, they seldom stay in the lake for more than a season – no doubt going over the dam during spates.

The policy of introducing rainbows on a regular basis – usually in mid-May – was restarted in 1973. John Baynes included some hefty rainbows at each stocking. This certainly increased the enjoyment of a day's fishing as one has set out with the knowledge that there is just a chance of getting into a 'big one'.

As an aside, 250 North American brook trout were stocked in 1966. Of these only 29 were taken and a further 37 in 1967 and then a blank. Probably a case of migration again, but those caught – I personally took several – fought like demons and seemed to thrive in Vyrnwy.

Encouraged by the partial success of the '66 experiment, it was decided to have another go at stocking 'brookies' in the spring of 1973, when a number were entered into Rhiwargor.

The North American brook trout is a delightfully shaped and marked fish with distinctive orange pectoral fin tips and green backs.

Brook trout returns were spectacular in 1981, 82 and 83 with a high proportion of those stocked being caught. However, the returns again dropped and it was decided to stop entering 'brookies'. Jim Talbot also put some into the lake in the late 1980's but the result proved a disappointment again.

Newly stocked trout are sometimes unkindly called 'factory fish' at Vyrnwy and are thought to be poor sport during the first few months while they become acclimatised to the different and harsher environment. However, never presume at the beginning of the season that all the new fish will take their time to settle down. Just as large rainbows are being entered into the lake now, the same is true of brown trout. They can give quite a shock in those early days to the unaware who expect nothing larger than a ten ouncer.

However, there is one complaint or observation from my fellow fishermen that is hard to refute. 'Factory fish' are hardly a patch on 'native' Vyrnwy trout when it comes to the breakfast table.

We find a marked difference in their appearance as well. It may take him a year to acquire the darker and more attractive hue of the home grown product. But some variation in colouring does occur depending on location.

Those from the top of Rhiwargor are often paler backed than those living just around the point under the laurels of Eunant. Fish lying under the many trees lining the banks, the Chapel beat for example, are distinctly dark, as are those of the deeper dam end.

Incidentally, on a flat calm day it is possible to lean over the dam wall and see fish swimming about near the surface in the summer. For those who cannot seem to get to terms with the Vyrnwy trout, this can be an encouragement. It shows that there are at least some fish in the lake!

Newcomers and guests often ask about the depth of a particular bay or drift. To the fisherman, it is important to know when the lake is full early in the season that Rhiwargor, most of Cedig, Llyn Rhiw and parts of Eunant are shallow and will probably be high and dry with a fair covering of vegetation by the end of the summer. The fish, on balance, prefer to live in this weedier environment, when the waters return.

On the other hand, the height from the old river bed of the dam to overflow level is 84 feet – so that is also the deepest part of the lake. You will see a steel buoy floating a hundred yards or so off the Boathouse Pool bridge below the Hotel. This is another deep hole as the buoy marks the lowest level that the Water Authority can take supplies in the event of severe drought stranding the straining tower.

Old hands at Vyrnwy use low water conditions to study the topography of the lake bed. All kinds of tumbled-down dry stone walls, bridges and buildings come to light and, when the lake is full, these are all good holding places for fish. It is worth studying the original course of the river in Rhiwargor in times of drought. The natural current, although hardly discernible, follows this path even today when Vyrnwy is at overflow level.

Mentioning Rhiwargor, bird lovers among anglers are in for a double bonus when fishing this arm of the lake. In 1977, the RSPB established the Lake Vyrnwy Reserve. This was created by the Severn-Trent Water Authority, the RSPB, the Forestry Commission, and the Lake Vyrnwy Hotel, as the sporting tenants, in an agreement in 1973. The Reserve covers 16,000 acres with the north west of the lake as a focus.

Dozens of varieties of water and upland bird life can be seen on the Reserve or from a boat. The most obvious sign of the RSPB presence is the new hide tucked away on the island at the top of the Rhiwargor arm of the lake. It is well signposted and is approached via an attractive lake-side woodland pathway.

*Historical Highlights*

Students of angling history will, I trust, find this section of some interest. It is really a potted narrative of Vyrnwy's fishing past since the first artificial fly was cast on to its waters in 1891.

Trout fishing started just two years after the lake was finally completed and the waters were at full level in 1889. The first fishing trial before the formal opening of the fishery took place on 3 February 1891. The result was most encouraging.

On the starting day, three trout were taken of good size – 1 lb 5 oz, 1 lb 3 oz and 1 lb 1 oz.

During the trial period covering February and the early part of March that year, many trout of over the pound mark were caught. Messrs W. H. Avery, H. B. Harvey, A. P. Thornley and G. Ward were the pioneers. They took thirty two fish weighing in total 29 lb 3 oz.

The various gentlemen suffered an almost endless 'blizzard' with complaints about difficulties in rowing boats in the prevailing conditions.

Fishing started in earnest on Good Friday 27 March 1891 in 'continuation of blizzard'. The beginning day attracted nineteen rods and in all 114 fish were caught weighing an average of over three quarters of a pound. Favourite flies during those first few months appear in the records as March Brown, Mallard and Claret and Mallard and Black. A trout of 2 lb was landed by 'The Turners'.

During 1891, a grand total of 4,143 trout were caught with an average weight of just under the pound. Mr G. Ward the first lessee of the hotel, proved top of the fishermens' league with some 258 trout working out at 222 lb 12 oz.

The Register was signed by 'Mr Durant Gibbings,

Manager'. Going back just a few years from then, the fame of the Vyrnwy River had certainly spread to Liverpool. An article in the 31 October 1885 edition of the *Fishing Gazette* entitled 'A wet day on the Vyrnwy' tells of some intrepid members of the Liverpool Angling Association who arrived by train at Llanymynech and 'shiveringly hastened to the Cross Keys'.

Although only on the river – the lake still far from completion – the party is reported in the article as spending most of their time having 'nips' and endless hot glasses 'or two'.

Trouting was in full swing on the lake during the 1890's. Captain G. H. France took the best fish of 1892 of 2 lb 6 oz and over 18 inches long.

Detailed records were again kept in 1893 with many trout of over a pound being taken. The largest fish caught that year was 2 lb 12 oz and the average weight of the 4,340 fish ending on the hotel tray was over 14 oz.

It was in 1983 that a great Victorian enthusiast Mr C. W. Gedney stayed at the Lake Vyrnwy Hotel and returned home to Bromley, Kent to write a book entitled *Angling Holidays in pursuit of Salmon, Trout and Pike*.

His work makes fascinating reading today. The following short passages from his book must be essential material for inclusion in the lake's angling history.

'The Lake teems with pound trout, and, although they are not so thick as to be 'squeezing each other on the bank' like Pat's salmon, yet they are plentiful enough to yield a good basket every day to anyone who can fish at all, with a two pounder, maybe at the head of the score. Yes, it is real good fishing, and I know of no other place where you can get anything like it.

There are two kinds of trout in the lake – the aboriginal brownies, and the 4,000 Loch Levens put in some years ago which have thriven amazingly.

What grand fighting fish of Loch Levens are! My little ten foot splitcane rod – on which I have killed many 3 lb chalk stream trout in May fly season – was no better than a child's toy against a pound Loch Leven in Lake Vyrnwy. I had to mount a substantial twelve footer, and even then some of the fish took as long to kill as a fresh run sea-trout.

The hotel is, in truth, replete with all the comforts of a well ordered house, and a man who comes here on fishing bent, can be taken in and done for at an inclusive charge of three and a half guineas per week. Of this comfortable hostelry some grateful anglers have written, with poetic fervour:

*We were out for a spin and we stopped at this Inn,*
*Where there's plenty of grub for inflating the skin,*
*The fishing was splendid; Miss Davies was good,*
*Stop if you can; we would if we could.*

The lady immortalised in the foregoing verse is the manageress and lessee of the establishment, and a real good one she is, too, and every grateful brother of the rod will testify who visits Lake Vyrnwy Hotel.'

Public relations may not have been invented in 1893 but Mr Gedney deserved a fat fee for that eulogy. Perhaps he got one!

One notable entry for 1894 appears in the entry for 3 September. I quote: 'Boatmen. 15 fish of total 12 lbs for Duke of York's Luncheon.'

The chub menace, still present today, was first tackled in 1898. The Register mentions that on Tuesday 14 June 'Chubbing started today. Killed 1,300 fish weighing one ton.' Chub still begin their spawning run in June and can often be seen in a large shoal at the head of Rhiwargor.

There was no 'limit' to the number of fish one could take in those early years. In 1899, the Rev Gregorie and boatman caught forty three fish in one day and Mr Garside topped this slaughter the next year with a colossal basket of forty five fish reaching 38 lb – 'the best yet made one lake'.

During the first decade, the average annual weight was around the 11 oz mark. A sharp drop to around 8 oz started in 1906 and lasted at this level until a major effort was made to improve the fishery, starting in 1929.

Stocking of the lake was re-introduced that year and a 9

inch 'limit' finally brought in. Four thousand brown trout were entered plus 1,000 rainbows.

The following March, Squadron-Leader Graham Martin, whose wife Belinda was the hotel's proprietor, took further positive, and, as it turned out, highly rewarding steps to upgrade the fishing.

The following passage is rather technical so perhaps an entomologist should be consulted for a further explanation. '100,000 Limnea Peregra and 20,000 Gammarus laid down in suitable tributaries and bays' on 25 March. Just a fortnight later, another 50,000 of the former were placed into the river at the top end and other tributaries.

Many tons of basic slag – a form of fertilizer – was dumped at the head of Rhiwargor to encourage the growth of plant life.

The outcome of all this expense and hard work proved highly gratifying. By 1934, the average weight was back to 10 oz and reached a satisfactory 13 oz by the outbreak of World War II. Satsifactory, I say, since in 1936 nine rainbows of over 3 lb were taken during the season. Quite a change in just six years.

The war meant a cessation of stocking for the duration, transport being the obvious problem. 'Soldiers may have taken considerable number of fish' is one terse comment in the Register. A further menace were the scores of cormorants which infested booms laid across the lake to deter flying-boats or torpedoes fired at the dam.

Catching a really large fish then became a rare event indeed – almost a once in a decade occasion.

That excellent, but now defunct, publication the *Fishing Gazette* carried many mentions of the lake Vyrnwy fishery over the years – there is even a small lake in the woods behind the Boathouse Pool named after the magazine.

An article that appeared in the 22 March 1913 edition of the *Fishing Gazette* by Mr Walter Gallichan covers a particular Vyrnwy phenomenon, the Coch y Bondhu or bracken beetle.

Gallichan also published a charming booklet about the fishing on the lake, entitled *Lake Vyrnwy and Around. An account of a Welsh Highland, its sports, scenery and associations*, in 1912.

Apart from showing the tariff at the hotel – at that time you could have fishing with boat and one man, including man's lunch and ale, seven shillings per day (35p new money) – and some delightful pictures of the interior of the hotel and lake – he desribes Vyrnwy as 'the Loch Leven of Wales'. He gives the reader a tour round the lake and it is fascinating that today's fish favour exactly the same places as their forebears 80 years ago. His book is valid in every respect as a guide to fishing the lake in 1992 – with the exception of the bracken beetle.

During the Fern-Web or Coch y bondhu season, from the end of June to about the third week of July, great execution may be done with the counterfeit fly. Mr Kennedy's floating beetle can be recommended in the Coch y bondhu season. It is a cunning imitation, and I speak from experience when I say that it is quickly seized by the trout in mistake for the real insect.

Writing about the 1930's, Sir Edward Durand is concerned about the future of the Coch y bondhu Beetle in his fascinating book *Wanderings With a Fly Rod*. This is a real treasure and contains the most sound advice on fishing, proper behaviour – including handling fish – and where to find trout. He wrote;

> I think the days I really enjoyed most were in late June and early July, when for a short time the Coch y bondhu beetle was coming off the hillside on to the water, but the fall of this tit-bit for the trout is a very chancey and uncertain event. The cork imitation, fished dry, of course, is a most amusing sport, and because of the weight, especially on fine gut, it is quite easy to break on the strike. Before the days of the increase of rainbows, which necessitated the use of stronger casts, it used to be quite a common event to leave the beetle in a fish's mouth, and as often as not he promptly spat it out again, and then commenced the boatman's great game of 'Hunt the Beetle'.
>
> I heard one amusing story first hand, from an exceedingly large and fine specimen of a fisherman, a veritable son of

Anak, who lost his beetle on the strike and, having spotted it later, discarded by the trout and floating on the surface was rowed down to recover it. Just as his large hand was extended to pick it off the water a hungry trout rose and took it from between his fingers, and his surprise jump was nearly enough to upset the whole boat load, much to the alarm of the other occupants. Of course to be a *real* fishing story he should have caught the fish in his hand!

Unfortunately, the intensive planting of coniferous trees all around the lake is, I fear, restricting and destroying the breeding-ground of the Coch y bondhu. Not only that but it is also seriously interfering with the sport of the inhabitants of the hotel who come in the Autumn and Winter months for the shooting, because the enormous forests are growing up without any rides or openings in them, making it impossible to beat them for game, besides harbouring all kinds of vermin which the keepers cannot get at to destroy.

The beetle is almost the May Fly of the lake, and its possible extinction would be a very serious loss. The Coch y bondhu dry fly is very often successful before and after a fall of the real beetle, and is generally quite the most useful dry fly all season through.

Edward Durand's concern for the Coch y bondhu has been fully justified. It is effectively gone and the last fisher, to my knowledge, to use the cork imitation with any success, apart from around the Tower during feeding time! – is Michael Horton Ledger. Until the forests are cleared and the open moor allowed back in their place, we will not see it reappear.

Incidentally, Durand's book started John Baynes and his father Sir Roy on their 'affair' with Lake Vyrnwy back in 1946.

The Coch y bondhu was a highly popular bait – either as a fly or floating cork replica – for many years, although 'out of fashion' today. Indeed, intrigued to see if it still worked, I called in at Hardy's, Pall Mall in the late 1970's and asked an elderly assistant if the shop had any in stock. He thought for a moment and said: 'I doubt if we have any left. The last time I sold any of those was before the last war to a gentleman that used to fish a place called Lake Vyrnwy in Wales!'

Writing an article entitled 'Lake Vyrnwy – an introduction to newcomers' in the slim-line wartime *Fishing Gazette* in 1944, Col Richard Page also had some good things to say about the Coch y Bondhu beetle.

But he also drew our attention back to the chub – which he did not like at all. He wrote 'A dry fly accepted by a chub is best sent to a dry cleaner if it is ever to float again. Chub are slimy to handle, difficult to kill and eject filthy green messes from both ends all over the boat in their death throes, and they eat much which would otherwise go to the trout.'

I have also written about the Vyrnwy chub, in the *Trout and Salmon* magazine a few years ago. My view was not quite so jaundiced since a 3 lb chub in deep water can put up a tough, if somewhat stolid, fight.

The Westropp family guide to the lake during those first chaotic outings in 1946/7/8 was Richard Threlfall's slim volume, entitled *Notes on Trout Fishing on Lake Vyrnwy and the Upper Vyrnwy River*. It was something of a bible to us and we were in great awe of the man. Although I was very young, I remember him snatching the ex-tank aerial rod being used by my mother and hurling it to the ground announcing grandly 'No man can fish with that'. He was right. For at that moment a car swung round the top bend on the drive and flattened the grey metal rod into spaghetti.

Back to trout and Dick Page caught a trout of just under 4 lb near the Tower in 1952. It was the biggest fish taken on Lake Vyrnwy for over thirty years.

His achievement was quickly topped – the following year Mr F. Ledsam landed a fish of 4 lb 10 oz. The largest caught since the fishery started, his record breaker was 23 inches long and 13 inches in girth.

All the same, the average weight still stayed below the half pound during the whole of the 1940's and 1950's.

The famous drought of 1959 caused alarmists among the experts to state that the lake would take at least two years to reach its full level once more. They were very wrong. Water was going over the dam again by mid-summer 1960.

An unofficial report is of a fish weighing a gigantic 7 lb 2 oz by Mr Norman Davies of Bala. He says he boated the 'whale' just below Cedig but there is nothing in the Register to verify the catch – even though the local paper records the achievement and Mr Davies assures us of its authenticity. It would seem likely – pure conjecture though – that this fish's normal habitat was round the Tower and he had swum up to Cedig in search of more food.

It was not until 1961, that the average weight rose above 8 oz again. Since then, the size of trout brought in has slowly but surely increased.

The average weight reach the 1 lb mark for the first time in 1978 which is mainly a credit to the excellent stocking policy. For example, 36 trout of over 2½ lbs were caught in 1979 plus a brown of 5½ lbs. Year followed year with the average weight approaching the magic 1 lb mark. The last decade has also been notable for big fish, frequently caught near the Tower.

The nationwide drought of 1976 hit Lake Vyrnwy even harder than the long dry spell of 1959. The fishing certainly suffered. But, with the water level down more than 32 feet, a number of features of the old drowned village of Llanwddyn – situated off Cedig – were exposed for the first time since 1889.

The ruins came into view again in the great drought of 1987. I spent a week at the hotel with my small sons Edward and Kit in August '87 and we spent hours exploring the empty lake bed in Eunant, off Cedig and virtually the whole of Rhiwargor.

1991 was a spectacular fishing year. The total catch was a record, just short of 3,000 fish, and a monster rainbow of 7 lbs 2 oz was taken. It was fitting that the centenary year should be such a good one.

*The Lake's Ecology*

When John Baynes took over the fishery at the beginning of 1973, he invited Dr Margaret E. Brown, who was then biologist to the Salmon and Trout Association, to visit Vyrnwy and write a report which he hoped would help him with future stocking policy.

In the event, Dr Brown's report covered a wide spectrum

of ecological and biological data. It made fascinating reading and reveals much about the lake and its inhabitants, fishy or otherwise, that was previously unknown or at best only guessed from experience.

So following are some key extracts from the report:

### Comments On The Fauna Collected

On 26 March, I visited sites round the Lake and three inflowing streams. At each sampling station, I examined stones and took a 'kick sample' with a pond-net; I examined the animals collected in a white pie-dish and noted what species I found and how abundant they were.

Samples from the lake shore where the substratum was stones and boulders or sand yielded few or no animals. This type of shore presents a harsh environment, particularly where there are changes in lake level. Much of the lake edge is of this type and will give very little in the way of food for trout.

Where the lake shore was of a more gentle slope, with muddy sand and stones and some plants growing on it, there were more animals than on stony shores.

Zooplankton was abundant in Rhiwargor and I caught two small chub at Heartbreak Bay; these were fat and had evidently found enough to eat. This type of lake shore will produce food for fishes though the fauna was not very rich. The fact that Rhiwargor Bay is considered a good fishing locality probably is related to the shallow water and greater productivity there.

Of the inflowing streams, Eunant proved very disappointing even up the valley where I had expected to find plenty of stonefly and flat mayfly nymphs. Cedig had a poor fauna where it was shaded by trees but the small stream sampled just above the woodland had an excellent fauna. The Rhirwargor stream and its tributary had fair faunas but the animals were much less abundant than in the small Cedig tributary. The Rhiwargor and upper Cedig should provide food and suitable spawning for trout (and chub in Rhiwargor); the Eunant seems almost useless as a nursery. The tiny stream flowing into Heartbreak Bay had a poor fauna but better than the Eunant.

There is likely to be an indigenous population, spawning in inflowing streams and moving into the lake after one or more years. Many of the streams are shaded and have a poor fauna. Eunant stream has a poor fauna in spite of not being shaded; this is probably because it is acid, at least at some times of year (since it is now recognised that streams with occasional pH values below 6 usually have a sparse fauna compared with similar streams with pH always above 6). It seems likely that the indigenous trout population is not very large – that is, it does not seem likely that the trout grow slowly because of overstocking.

I have annual lengths calculated from scales read by Dr Worthington in 1939:

| Age in years | 1 | 2 | 3 | 4 | 5 | 6 |
|---|---|---|---|---|---|---|
| Length (inches) | 1.8 | 3.9 | 6.8 | 9.0 | 10.3 | 11.6 |

(based on 10 fish)

This indicates a growth rate slower than in Bala (Llyn Tegid) where the fish reach 8½ inches at three years old and 10½ at four.

Trout growth rates are very much dependent on food supply. My investigations showed that the food supply in the lake is very limited since much of the shore in unproductive and changes in water level must limit the productivity of the gently sloping, sandy-mud shores. There may at times be plenty of zooplankton but Vyrnwy with its soft water is likely to be unproductive of plankton and zooplankton is good food for smaller rather than larger trout. The main source of food for large trout must be of terrestrial origin – blown off the surrounding land; this food also will encourage the fish to rise to flies cast be anglers.

Rough pasture with heather and bracken is quite a good source of terrestrial insects of trout food. Plantations of conifers are a very poor source because foresters naturally try to keep the numbers of insects as low as possible. Beech and rhododendron are other species which produce few insects and so are not useful as sources of food for trout. The present use of the Vyrnwy catchment, mainly for forestry and largely for conifers, must have reduced the amount of terrestrial food available compared with the rough pastures that surrounded the lake until the 1930's.

There is evidence from some continental streams that plantations of red cedar and Sitka and Norway spruce produce substances that are toxic to insects, possibly also to trout so that trout are scarce and grow slowly in streams flowing through these plantations and for several miles below them. It may be that the plantations of spruce round Vyrnwy are discouraging the trout – but the volume of water in the lake is so large that I do not think this can be an important effect. Streams flowing through these plantations would be no use as nurseries for trout.

# CHAPTER SEVEN

## How To Fish the Lake

*By G. V. Westropp*

This chapter is primarily aimed at anglers of limited experience or those who have never, or seldom, cast a fly on Lake Vyrnwy. I hope that fishers who know the water or those with experience of loch and mountain stream fishing will not find this particular section patronising.

The key word to all fly fishing is commonsense. And there is no substitute for local knowledge. The more one gets to 'understand' a lake or river, the better will be the reward.

Put your flies where it seems logical that trout would lie, use correct tackle, and suitably sized and patterned flies. Make sure you have a strong enough – but not too heavy – 'leader' or cast and fish the line at a speed you think best in prevailing conditions.

All pretty obvious stuff, you think. But I have been out with a fellow angler who, despite exhortations from an expert boatman and myself, insisted that we drift straight down the centre of the lake opposite Cedig. Being a guest, I could do nothing and became considerably frustrated with that inviting bay a couple of minutes row away. The result of a hard day's flogging was nothing. Another boat hugging the bank came home with a bag of five brace – all caught in two hours!

Take advice. Ask. It costs nothing and can make all the difference. There will always be somebody about who has experience of the lake. Ask at the Hotel, another fisherman, or a boatman. You will find information more than readily available, although I must admit everybody seems to have different theories. No matter, as long as they produce trout.

Find out what size and pattern of fly is likely to be the most effective in the prevailing conditions, where you should fish, etc. The list of questions is endless.

Keep your flies in the water as much as possible. I suppose this is the best bit of advice of all. You will not catch a thing if your rod is lying idle in the boat or on the bank.

That great boatman the late Sim Carpenter was a real tyrant in this respect. He taught me and dozens of others practically everything we know about fishing the lake. To put your rod down for half a second brought a sharp rebuke. Result – exhaustion, a very tired wrist, and a good number of fish.

The actual technique you should use in your quest for the Vyrnwy trout can vary almost as much as the weather.

Here are some basic guidelines.

*Casting*

In conditions permitting any sort of reasonable drift, cast a fairly short line. The reasons for this are several. The fisherman has closer contact with any taking trout, and he is easier to control when hooked. More casts are possible per minute and therefore more water covered. It is a great deal less work – especially in a high wind – and very much safer for your partner in the boat.

In contrast to the above, I sometimes cast a long line fished fast. But then I invariably fish alone and practice the dangerous habit of standing in the boat. This is definitely not recommended unless you happen to be both agile and on your own boat.

When with others, cast ahead of you or at any rate cover the water in your sector. Do not poach your partner's zone or whisk your flies over his or her head – or the boatman's.

Concerning poaching, never interfere with another boat's drift or disturb the water which he may be over a few minutes later. It is the height of bad manners.

'Wetting the flies' is often given as an excuse for trolling when rowing up or motoring to take position to start a drift. I can see nothing wrong with this but a far more effective form is to 'cast out and round'. Basically this entails casting a longish line out at ninety degrees from the boat as it is being rowed and only retrieving when it has completely straightened out behind you. The final twitch of the fly is as it turns to straighten is most attractive to the trout.

The classic loch-style cast for a boat – only boat fishing is normally allowed on Lake Vyrnwy – is a mainly repetitive process. Cast out the length of line that you find most comfortable in the conditions and then 'fish' your flies. Start retrieving them almost as soon as the line lands on the water in an insect or minnow-like fashion. This is done by small upward movements of the tip of the rod at the same time as pulling in line by hand.

Other favour a smooth and constant retrieval of line. Either way, the flies move attractively through the water and you maintain the essential contact with them – thus the anglers' traditional good luck 'tight lines' pleasantry.

Developments in rod and line manufacturing and the recent explosion in the number of reservoirs – particularly in England – that are chiefly fished from the bank has led to the evolvement of a third style of casting.

'Double haul' and 'shooting head' are now common expressions among trout fishermen. Basically, they refer to the technique of aerialising many yards of line to achieve casting distances unthinkable a few years ago.

A good reservoir bank fisherman with the modern graphite rod and tackle can fairly comfortably land a fly 30 or even 40 yards away. And traditionalists who thought that the new methods would 'never answer' at Vyrnwy have been in for a surprise. Many fish have been killed by the 'super casters' since they first appeared at the lake in the mid-1970's when other anglers have come home fishless.

Of course, flies can be fished in the old fashioned manner after an ultra long cast if the boat is drifing very slowly in a gentle breeze. But things are seldom that simple.

'Stripping' line back into the boat smoothly and fast is the usual method – overcoming the problem of a quick drifting boat.

The 'supercast' was not developed for boat fishing. It evolved as a direct result of overcrowded reservoir bank fishing. Just look at a picture of the most English reservoirs in the angling press, famous waters like Grafham, Rutland and Bewl Bridge, and you will see fishermen standing shoulder to shoulder like so many herons. They have to belt out great lengths of line as wading and floundering anglers have frightened the trout away from the lake margins.

My personal view is that fishing with a shooting head and then stripping in yards of line like some demented mackerel fishermen is dull stuff. But the fast moving flashing lure does catch fish at Vyrnwy when the traditionalists often fail.

## Rods

Nowhere in the game sports, fishing, shooting, stalking or hunting, has there been such a revolution in basic equipment as among salmon and trout rods. Indeed, the introduction of the carbon fibre or new graphite rod is a spin-off from space technology.

The profound effect on casting techniques of the new rods has been covered in the preceding section. The key to the success of carbon fibre and graphite as materials for fly rods, or indeed all fishing rods, is their strength and lightness.

The majority of fly anglers who have been fishing for 30 years or more still own split cane rods and they are treasured possessions to remember earlier outings. But they feel very heavy after a season using a man-made material counterpart.

I still have all my split cane Hardy's and Sharpe trout rods, some inherited from parents and even grandparents, hanging in my rod cupboard.

On winter evenings, they will occasionally be taken out of their cases and put together – I am afraid that is all the action they now see all year. Perhaps sadly, the 'lightweights' have taken over completely in my family as active rods.

For Lake Vyrnwy, and indeed the river as well, I recommend a rod of not more than nine feet. But an 8 foot 6 incher is quite adequate for Vyrnwy. They are easy on the wrist, can handle a good sized trout – I have killed a ten pound salmon on my original Hardy's eight and a half foot 'Jet' – and cast a surprisingly long line.

'Purists' still prefer to 'shortline' for mountain lake fish in Wales, Scotland and Ireland. This technique uses only a few feet of actual fly line on each cast with a long leader. The team of flies, with the possible exceptions of the tail lure, stays on the surface during each short cast. The essential element is a bushy bob fly – a green peter, blue bottle or bibio etc. – which is dragged across the surface worrying the water. Fish will often follow the bob fly right up to the side of the boat before taking it or turning back onto the flashier mid or tail fly. Ideally, a longer rod of 10 or 11 feet is used to enable the fisher to work the team of flies as close as possible to the boat at the end of a cast. Sea trout, in particular, react well to short lining.

Remember when choosing a rod that you may well be fishing all day and the wrist and arm will take quite a hammering. Generally the lighter the rod you pick, the better. This is also even the case with longer rods for short lining.

*Lines and Reels*

What also matters, whether you are fishing at Vyrnwy or anywhere else, is the line and reel you use with your particular rod. A properly balanced rod will make casting a pleasure or will help enormously if you are still learning the art. Too big or small a reel will affect the whole action of the rod resulting in 'birds nests' tangles and lines landing on the water like depth charges – guaranteeing to put down every trout for yards around.

Modern rods have marks just above the butt showing exactly the correct weight of line to ue, e.g. # # 7. This means that the ideal line for this rod should carry a label on the packaging AFTM # # 7. Line weights under modern coding range from very light AFTM 3 up to salmon weight AFTM 12. (AFTM is the code of the Association of Fishing Tackle Manufacturers).

There is an added complication today for the unwary as lines are scientifically produced to do different jobs – nymph and dry fly, wet fly, fast sink, slow sink, sink tip only, the whole variety with double tapers so that they may be reversed to avoid excessive damage, weight forward and even lead core 'shooting heads' for ultra quick sink fishing.

This all sounds terrifying complicated and I certainly use different lines for different seasons on Vyrnwy – but only three.

Early spring sees the trout patrolling several feet below the colder surface water. A sinking line – for my rod an AFTM 7 double taper slow sinker – gets the team of flies down to their notice.

As the weather improves, the fish move up closer to the top for their feed and I switch reels to a floating double tapered line with a sink tip. By this I mean that the first 10 feet or so will take the cast down a foot or two almost immediately. The remainder of the line stays afloat for easy lifting and re-casting. There is nothing more infuriating to the 'wet' fisherman than to see his cast charging across the surface making bow waves like so many miniature speed boats.

The sunk tip is my key Vyrnwy and loch fishing line and I use it 80 per cent of the season.

Lastly, there are many occasions when you will want to fish a dry fly or a nymph. Here, the floating line comes into its element.

Just to confuse, the manufacturers now produce lines of almost every colour – green, grey, blue, brown, white and even peach shades are on offer. Each company will tell you in its promotional literature that their particular brand colour is least frightening to the fish.

I use either Masterline or the Cortland 444 peach range, but there are many first rate brands including Hardy, Air Cel, Leeda and Bob Church, Wetcel, Airflow and Shakespeare.

An American invention, the 'plastic' line has almost totally taken over from the trusty silk variety. They do not require drying or dressing, although wipe them down with a cloth every so often to remove mud and grease to ensure free-running through the top ring of the rod.

Look after your fly line – it is not a cheap item and with proper care will last for years.

*Casts or 'Leaders'*

Traditionally, fishermen use three flies in a team to fish Vyrnwy and similar waters. Therefore, the majority of casts on sale have two droppers – branches of nylon – tied onto the main piece of cast.

When I was learning to fish, my father banned droppers from the family boat – there were often five of us trying to fish at once – in an effort to cut down inevitable muddles and as a safety precaution.

His solution was either use a single fly or tie all three straight onto a length of nylon straight from a spool. When a general knitting happened, we would cut all the flies clear, dumped the useless nylon in a bag set aside for the purpose and tied up a new leader. This was much quicker than untangling the muddle and, because the nylon came off a spool, could be done reasonably cheaply. Cutting up bought ready-made up casts would have been an expensive exercise.

The 'dropperless dropper' leader is, I now gather, called a Dunkeld cast in the Highlands of Scotland.

The vast body of trout anglers still view my method of attaching flies with scepticism. That is fair enough because you must have faith in the tackle that you use.

As with lines, all fishing cast or clear nylon that can be made up into a leader has a clearly marked number on the packaging, e.g. 2.5 kg or 5 1b. This means the breaking strain of the material.

At Vyrnwy, I never use less than 4 lb breaking strain and usually 5 lb if I am fishing among the weeds at the top of Rhiwargor. Anything less may well lead to the frustrating experience of being broken by a good fish or losing the whole cast in a bunch of weed or grass or rocks.

*Flies*

For many readers, this will be the most important section of the book.

'What fly should I use' is the most frequently asked question of Jim Talbot – or indeed any proprietor of a fishing hotel – during the course of a season.

A list of flies that have attracted trout on Lake Vyrnwy over the yers would probably outstrip even the Hardy's catalogue.

However, for simplicity, I have made a selection of wet and dry flies, nymphs, as well as lures, to suit every taste, and I hope the trouts' as well. They have been split into patterns that have been consistently more successful at the different times of the season.

## Wet Flies

*Butcher*
Black wing, silver body and red tail

*Zulu*
Black hackle and body. Red tag.

*Peter Ross*
Teal wing, red and silver body. Golden pheasant tail.

*Coachman*
White wing, brown hackle. Peacock hurl body.

*Invicta*
Brown wing, yellow body and Blue throat.

*Teal and Green*
Teal wing, green body. Golden pheasant tail.

*Alexandra*
Peacock green wing, silver body and red tail. Jungle cock eye optional.

*Fry Fly*
Black hackle, white body. Peacock and red back and tag.

*Bibio*
Black body and hackle with dark red mid-body band.

## Lures

*Montana*
Black cock hackle black chenille body and fluorescent green throat.

*Sweeney Todd*
Black wing, magenta throat, black and silver body.

*Muddler Minnow*
Spun deer's hair nose, brown wing and gold body.

*Viva*
Black cock hackle wings, black chenille body and fluorescent green wool tail.

## Nymphs

*Yellow Sedge*
Pheasant tail cover,

*Pheasant Tail Nymph*
Pheasant tail cover,

brown hackle, brown or yellow body

*Black Buzzer*
Black body with silver rib. White head tuft.

body and tail

*Corixa*
Pheasant tail back, yellow body with silver rib.

## *Early Spring (March-April)*

*Wet*

Butcher
March Brown
Peter Ross
Invicta
Alexandra
Bibio
Zulu
Mallard and Claret
Black Pennell
Delphi

*Lures*

Viva
Sweeney Todd
Muddler Minnow
Black Chenille
Baby Doll

## *Spring – Early Summer (May-June)*

*Wet*

Zulu
Black and Peacock Spider
Invicta
Peter Ross
Teal and Green
Mallard and Claret
Coachman
Black Pennell
Green Peter

*Lures*

Viva
Muddler Minnow
Whisky fly
Montana

*Nymphs*

Pheasant Tail
Sedge Pupae
Black Buzzer

*Dry*

Greenwell's Glory
G and H Sedge
Sedges (various)

Demoiselle Nymph        Coch y Bondhu
Corixa                  Dry Pheasant Tail
Olive Nymph             Coachman

*Summer – Early Autumn (July-August-September)*

*Wet*                   *Lures*

Butcher                 Viva
Invicta                 Sweeney Todd
Peter Ross              Muddler Minnow
Coachman                Whisky Fly
Black Pennell           Baby Doll
Blue Zulu               Black Chenille
Mallard and Claret      Montana
Alexandra
Bibio

*Nymphs*                *Dry*

Pheasant Tail           Greenwell's Glory
Sedge Pupae             G and H Sedge
Buzzers (red and black) Coch y Bondhu

As you will see, there are some patterns that are fished throughout the season. The Butcher, Peter Ross and Invicta among the wet flies and lures like the Viva and Muddler Minnow will be as good as any other from March through till September.

But there is always one pattern each month that is 'in vogue'. A successful fisherman reports back that he has taken all his fish on a 'Green Wonder' or whatever and everybody else immediately adds the fly to their team.

The odds in favour of that particular fly working therefore automatically rise. It will stay the favourite until somebody else makes a killing on a 'Black Wonder' and the whole process happens all over again.

My advice is fish the 'in' fly but never abandon the traditionally successful patterns solely for the newcomer.

One rule drummed into me by an old fisherman was 'bright flies for a bright day'. There may be some substance to this but, looking back through my own fishing book, I can find no conclusive evidence on this one.

What size of fly to use is another question frequently asked. Size 10 or 12, judging by results, would appear to be right for Lake Vyrnwy and most mountain lochs.

*Playing a Fish*

When you hook a trout, the first and most important rule is try and keep in contact with him by applying a firm yet steady pressure.

While remembering that your 'cast' is not a rope hawser, do not be too frightened to impose your will on the fish. If you let the line go slack or delay too long in bringing the fish to the net, you should not be surprised to find your quarry gone.

Keep the rod tip up to ensure maximum pressure on the fish. This will tire him far more quickly and stop a crash dive to the safety of weed or other underwater snags.

However, if your trout, particularly a rainbow, leaps clear of the water during the 'battle' immediately lower the tip of the rod in order to avoid getting 'broken'. A useful hint this, and one I have several times ignored to my cost.

Lastly, play your fish to a degree where it is possible to net him easily – without delaying too long.

*Netting*

Netting is an art. The rule here is never jab at the fish. Slide the net quietly under him and gently lift the net clear of the water.

Jabbing can lead to smashed casts, snagged flies or frighten the fish in a fresh hectic run for freedom.

Next, killing your catch. A sharp tap about an inch above his nose should be enough. Do not beat his brains out and certainly do not thrust your thumb down his throat and bend back his head until the neck breaks. This technique may be fine for a cod fish but is undignified for the game trout.

*Boats*

As I have mentioned, all fishing on Vyrnwy is from a boat. A number of the whalers used on the lake today are the original 1890's article and have survived because they are ideal for the job and have been lovingly maintained and refurbished each winter for almost 100 years.

Boats are available from the Boathouse Pool at the dam end and the Rhiwargor boats are moored half a mile from the top of the Lake at 'Whitegates'.

Cedig, that favourite spot of many fishermen, also holds several boats. This means that every inch of the 11 mile shore line is now readily accessible to the angler.

A word here about tying up boats when you come off the water at the end of an outing. Always double check that the chain or rope is utterly secure. So many boats have been smashed to bits on the rocks overnight simply because people either forgot, or did not bother, to tie them firmly to the Boathouse Pool railing or the concrete blocks provided.

Stow the oars so that the blades are inside the boat and out of danger. Oars are expensive items today and a little care at the end of the day will prolong their life.

Many Vyrnwy fishers now prefer to hire the hotel's excellent and silent running electric outboards to get around the Lake. Their introduction – against much initial opposition from old stagers like myself – has revolutionised fishing on the Lake. There is now no part of the shore line that is too far to reach.

However, remember the following golden rules. Always think of the storage capacity of the battery before motoring off grandly three miles or so down wind. Vyrnwy batteries go flat like any others. Rowing a boat against a strong wind and rough wave for several miles is not recommended. Never switch on the engine with a line nearby in the water. Thousands of expensive lines have been wound around propellers to destruction. The Lake has a rocky shore line so think of the propeller whenever starting from the mooring point or nearing the bank. The drive shaft flips up easily out of the water with minimum effort and use oars when first getting underway or just before docking.

9   Graham Martin in a butt on the grouse moors with his spaniel Don

10   Billy Thomas in his chauffeur's cap standing beside the Martin's Rolls-Royce in 1939. Don the spaniel enjoys a perch on the running-board

11 Jamie Moir in 1953

12 Ruth Moir in 1953 with Benty, Sal, and her first litter of puppies

13 Taken in the 1960s. In front is Sim Carpenter, doyen of Lake Vyrnwy boatmen. The fisherman is Michael Horton Ledger, who has known the hotel all his life, having first come to stay with his parents in the 1930s

14 John Hill, farm bailiff

15  John Thomas, Ida Thomas, Alice Carpenter, and Miriam Probert standing outside The Tavern in about 1970

16  Bob Roberts, boatman. The son-in-law of Tom Hughes, and father of Brian, now head gamekeeper in 1992

17   A group of motor-cycle enthusiasts outside the hotel in the 1930s. Graham Martin is seated on someone's side-car on the right of the picture

18　Members of the Tanners' Club about to set off on their motor-cycles from the hotel in 1991. In front Peter Sheen holds a bottle of Tanners claret presented by Richard Haydon, a director of the wine merchants

19  Head keeper and three regular pickers-up. From the left: George Evans, Mrs Mabel Roberts, Alwyn Hughes and Brian Roberts

Some fishers are rightly nervous about fishing from a boat on a large expanse of water and life jackets are available from the hotel.

*General*

Fishermen employing the untiring services of the excellent boatmen should – need I say it – be considerate. They have a hard job often sitting all day in pouring rain, sleet or snow while you are hopefully enjoying yourself. A good 'dram' at the end of the day, apart from a lunchtime beer or two, is much appreciated.

Listen to their wise words but never allow yourself to be over bullied by their enthusiasm for you to catch a 'limit'. As I have already said, it can be a very tiring business!

The 'limit' for some years past has been four brace a day (8 fish) and no fish under 10 inches is allowed to be killed. In the case of an undersized trout that must be put back, do so as gently as you are able.

Hold him in a wet rag as our body temperature is considerably higher than a trout's and human contact must be a searing experience. The less damage done to his mouth and gills, the more likely he will grow big enough to take you on again another day.

Those intending to fish alone should know how to handle boats, be able to swim and have some fly-fishing experience. Also, rowing along back to your boat station against a howling gale may prove impossible. It has happened to me.

A useful gadget when fishing on your own to help maintain a drift without the endless interruption of straightening the boat is the 'drogue'. This simple device acts like a parachute in the water and is cheap. Just drop it behind the boat on some strong cord and it will slow your drift by 50 per cent.

Landing nets should have as long a handle as possible. I use a Hardy's model with a large net mouth and telescopic handle. Just remember to extend the handle before starting to fish! Fighting both a fish and the landing net at the same time is highly frustrating.

'Priests' – instruments for knocking trout on the head – can be made of almost any material. A short stout piece of wood will do the job as well as the professionally made article. Never use the side of the boat. Voices do not put trout down but crashes and bangs in the boat certainly do.

If you arrive at the lake without an essential bit of tackle, there is no necessity to despair. The hotel has an excellent supply of virtually everything you will require.

Rods are also on offer as well as a range of lines. Trays containting a wide selection of suitable flies can be inspected. Again, ask if you are not sure what to use. The same applies to casts, or 'leaders'.

*Weather and Clothing*

Weather conditions at Vyrnwy can change with alarming rapidity. They can be appalling or brilliant. The valley appears to have a weather pattern all of its own. It can be pouring with rain at Vyrnwy and bright sunshine just nine miles down the hills at Llanfyllin or vice versa.

It can further be completely different at the same time one end of the lake from the other.

Basically, Vyrnwy is a rainy place. I doubt the Liverpool Corporation would have chosen the valley as a reservoir if this were not so. The average annual rainfall there during the years 1916–50 was an impressive 75 inches. Poor Rhiwargor gets – again on average – 12 inches more rain per year than the dam end.

Winds are so variable that they can change direction several times a day. At the Eunant–Rhiwargor point by the 'Oaks', the wind can hit you from two directions at once creating rather confusing fishing conditions. It can blow so hard with little warning that keeping the flies on – let alone in – the water takes a fair amount of skill. Handling the boat during these blows is sometimes hazardous.

And then inexplicably and infuriatingly the wind will die altogether and a mirror-like quality overtakes the lake. Casting becomes a delicate art and the trout enjoy a first rate view of everything you do.

The unpredictability of the wind at Vyrnwy is due to a combination of its geographical lie – south east to north west

– and the many gaps in the surrounding hills. So while the blow may be up the lake from the dam end, it may be coming in exactly the opposite direction down Eunant or Rhiwargor.

An unnecessarily gloomy picture may have been painted here. On the other side of the coin, I assure you that Vyrnwy pulls some really spectacular warm cloudless weeks and even months out of the bag.

Unfortunately, we fishermen seldom have the opportunity to get away from our various occupations to enjoy the best of the weather. So come prepared for anything from a heatwave to a blizzard.

Sou'westers, a warm and waterproof jacket or coat, mackintosh trousers and wellington boots are all mandatory equipment.

Leave your waders at home. You will not need them. They are dangerous in a boat – fall overboard with them on and you can sink like a stone.

The trout of Lake Vyrnwy frankly do not care two hoots what you look like. No fashion parade is warranted in either torrential rain or the hot spells.

## A Fishing Tour of the Lake

The Boathouse Pool will be the first encounter with the lake for most fishers – especially if the water level is high. Row a couple of strokes up the pool and then let the boat drift quietly, casting under the bushes and trees at either side. When the lake is full, the shallows at the top end of the BHP are especially rewarding.

Motoring or rowing out from the pool under the bridge into the main body of the lake, I am going to take you on an anti-clockwise tour of the shore line.

A rock promontory juts out into the lake just 100 yards from the bridge and you should be prepared for fish almost immediately. There is a gravelly beach around the point and the water is all worth fishing from there up to and including the Tower. Always cast as close as you can to the shore line and this will prove doubly important when there are overhanging branches.

The Tower always holds substantial numbers of fish on the

down-wind side of the arches linking the structure of the road. Occasionally, the Tower Keeper feeds the fish and it attracts a large, hungry shoal which lurks expectantly below. You may be lucky enough to witness feed time early in the year when literally hundreds of fish are thrashing on the surface looking for the pellets thrown down from above. Catching one of these fish can be much harder than it looks. The fish are lightning quick and spot the difference between your fly and a floating trout pellet. But it can be done and some very large fish have been brought back to the slab this way.

There are devotees of the Tower who will work patiently all day – sometimes fishing very deep. Some of the heaviest bags are caught this way.

If the wind is south or east, the next 100 yards after the Tower will be worth attention. I have seldom had much success over the next ¾ of a mile and tend to row straight on to within 400 yards of the next bay – Cedig. The water shallows and many fish hold round Cedig Bay, one of the stocking points around the lake. Later in the Spring, this will be a good place for rainbows.

Cedig Bay itself can be outstanding. My sister Maggie Vaux and I had 17 fish in an hour one morning in March and the water always holds a good head of trout. Again, fish as close as you can to the shore line and it is always worth pushing a line right into the bushes where the Cedig River enters the lake.

Out of Cedig and heading onwards, the shore line is shallow and can be good at all times of the year. Fish it thoroughly until arriving half a mile later at Llechwedd-du or Mrs Morris's Beach. Pay close attention to this whole area and particularly off the beach. Incidentally, when you have fished the area thoroughly it is a useful place for a picnic or respite from the elements.

The next important bay for the fisher is called Finnant, which is a further ¾ of a mile up the shore. Two small streams enter the lake here and I seldom drift it without at least one taker. The bushes as you round the corner towards the Chapel and Chapel Drift are worth covering.

The Chapel has been a favourite of mine for decades in the

evening. While it holds many small fish, there is invariably some movement under the trees and try to fish as close into the rocks as you can.

From there to the boat station as Whitegates should also be covered, but do not dally until you get to a large larch tree leaning out over the water at the start of the White Gates Beach. Beach may be too grand a word since it is covered in bush and alder. Here is another stocking point and it will hold fish all year round.

Just round the trees from the Whitegates boat station is a bay which every boat covers when setting out for the day from the top end of the lake. They are right to do so in all conditions.

When the lake is low, the top 400 yards of the lake will be almost unfishable, but when water allows, thoroughly cover the whole of the top end from Bailey's Point to the Island. It holds more fish than anywhere else on the lake – with the possible exception of around the Tower. Being shallow, you can drift right across the middle and never be more than 4 or 5 feet from the lake bed. Fish will take anywhere.

One of the best drifts is to line yourself up with the end of Bailey's Point if the wind is coming from the south or east and drift into the reeds – or vice versa for a west wind.

Rhiwargor is the most scenic arm of the lake and is a firm favourite with many regulars – including myself. The cliffs of Eunant Moor to the south and the northern bluffs around Allt-Forgan are more reminiscent of the Canadian Rockies than mid-Wales.

The upper Vyrnwy River enters Rhiwargor top left and holds many good trout. The numerous fry spawned and hatched in the river are a rewarding diet for larger fish and these potential cannibal fish are easily identifiable by their larger heads and long streamlined shape. A drift into and around the upper Vyrnwy River mouth can prove rewarding with a favourable wind.

The south shore of Rhiwargor, on the other hand, is tempting but fairly non-productive. I recommend rowing or motoring straight down to the point joining Rhiwargor and Eunant. Oak trees hang over the rock point and there are always fish under the trees. The Oaks are a favourite of many of the lakes' top fishers, including Michael Horton Ledger and Judge Bailey. These two teamed up for nearly 20 Easters and invariably come in with full baskets despite gales, hail or freezing rain. Their boatman, Ronnie Carpenter – the son of my tutor Sim – still fishes the lake and is a superb source of local knowledge if you are lucky enough to meet him.

Around the corner and into Eunant I find the right hand shore line disappointing. However, you will notice an island covered in small bushes at the top end near the road bridge. This is the site of Lord Powys' hunting lodge before the flooding a hundred or so years ago and the fish appear to enjoy the shallow water and the rocks among the ruins.

To the south of the road bridge, rhododendron bushes grow for two or three hundred yards and this is a favourite haunt of rainbows in the late Spring and early Summer. Work along the bushes and back out to the Hall ruins.

If the sun is shining, the drift from the Eunant road bridge out the half mile along the shore to the main body of the lake can be spectacular for native browns. In May, fish can move to virtually every cast and a dry fly flicked under the overhanging branches can work well. Because of the lie of this arm of the lake, the wind can blow in three or four directions in just a few minutes or just flat clam. It is difficult to get a regular drift, but the innovation of electric motors or the services of a ghilly or colleague to row quietly along prove invaluable.

Out into the lake again, the shore is very steep with high rocks running straight up to the road. Although the water is obviously deep, the drift from there up to Llyn Rhiw is another good location for native browns. It looks uninviting and most fishers pass it by. This is a mistake especially under the rhododendron bushes.

When the native browns start to move in late April, May and early June, the Eunant–Llywn Rhiw drift can be most exciting. I have had several baskets of 15 fish or more in an afternoon working this stretch.

Llywn Rhiw is shallow and you may discover fish across the whole bay. On windy days, it can be a useful haven but it is not a place to run out of battery power if you have set out from any of the normal boat stations. Crossing the lake on a windy day can be quite alarming with waves three or four feet high.

I have never caught a fish up in the river mouth of the bay so concentrate on the drift between the river and the large culvert some 300 yards down lake.

Given reasonable wind conditions, the long mile and a half drift from there to Ceunant Bridge with its waterfall is good for browns and well worth working down. To get your bearings, Ceunant Bridge/waterfall is almost exactly opposite Cedig Bay at the widest part of the lake.

Drifting on for the next half mile until Heartbreak Bay is unremarkable. There are always fish, but nothing spectacular. So called because it looks so intriguing and fishy Heartbreak Bay may have its fans but seldom comes up to expectations. I avoid it.

We are now drifting on to approach some rocks before turning the corner to Cownwy Tunnel and the Corporation Boat House. However, it also features a launching ramp for canoes and other water sport activities. It is a little disconcerting to find yourself surrounded by young people in bright orange canoes while drifting, as you think, quietly and peacefully along.

My usual routine is to move straight on to the dam and, if lucky, discover the foam lines some 10 or 12 feet from the dam wall. Rainbows seem to lurk below the foam line eating dead flies and other food blown down the lake. One afternoon fishing with Ned Kelly of Duncton Mill, we had six fish in 20 minutes casting straight into the twig and leaf filled foam. It is always a good idea to spend some minutes casting right up to the dam wall with a long line and fishing slowly and steadily back to the boat.

From the dam to the next tunnel – the Marchnant – can be uncomfortable since it is alongside the road where most visitors to Lake Vyrnwy first park before driving round. You can be assured of an appreciative audience – if that is what you enjoy.

The Marchnant Tunnel area is invariably worth a cast or two. At high water and exactly opposite the tunnel mouth, you can see a pin prick of white light from the other end of the tunnel a mile and a half through the mountain under the hotel. Incidentally, the Marchnant pool at the other end of the tunnel is a useful standby if conditions of the lake are too rough. It holds some surprisingly good fish, which are often trout who were too exhausted to continue back to the lake after their spawning run up the various streams.

We are now within half a mile of the Boathouse Pool again and the end of the round Lake Vyrnwy tour. Fish can be found around every yard of the 12 mile shore line. A final tip. Do resist the temptation to fish in the middle of the lake, with the exception of the shallows at the top of Rhiwargor or around the island at the top of Eunant. You will probably waste your time.

*The River*

Fishing the Upper Vyrnwy River from just below the dam to the bridge on the Cownwy Road is a totally different proposition from the lake.

And sadly, the quality of the fishing has declined during the last eight years.

While the lake is artificial, the level and flow rate of water in this stretch of the river is even more so. Under statute, the Severn-Trent Water Authority used to be required to release a large gallonage from the lake into the river during the first week of each month as 'compensation water'. This served to maintain something like natural conditions and literally flushed out the river.

However, Lake Vyrnwy has now become a 'balancing reservoir' with a more regular but smaller outflow of water into the river. New valves were installed in the dam in the middle 1980's which stopped any fish escaping through them, which was possible previously.

Only a few years ago, the level of the river would suddenly rise on 'compensation' day turning the peaceful tree-lined river into a boiling torrent. The other time it changed from a quiet, rock strewn stream into near spate followed prolonged rain, when large quantities of water cascaded over the dam wall. But alas, this is no longer the case.

The lack of rain during the past three years has combined with the Severn-Trent policy of keeping water levels below

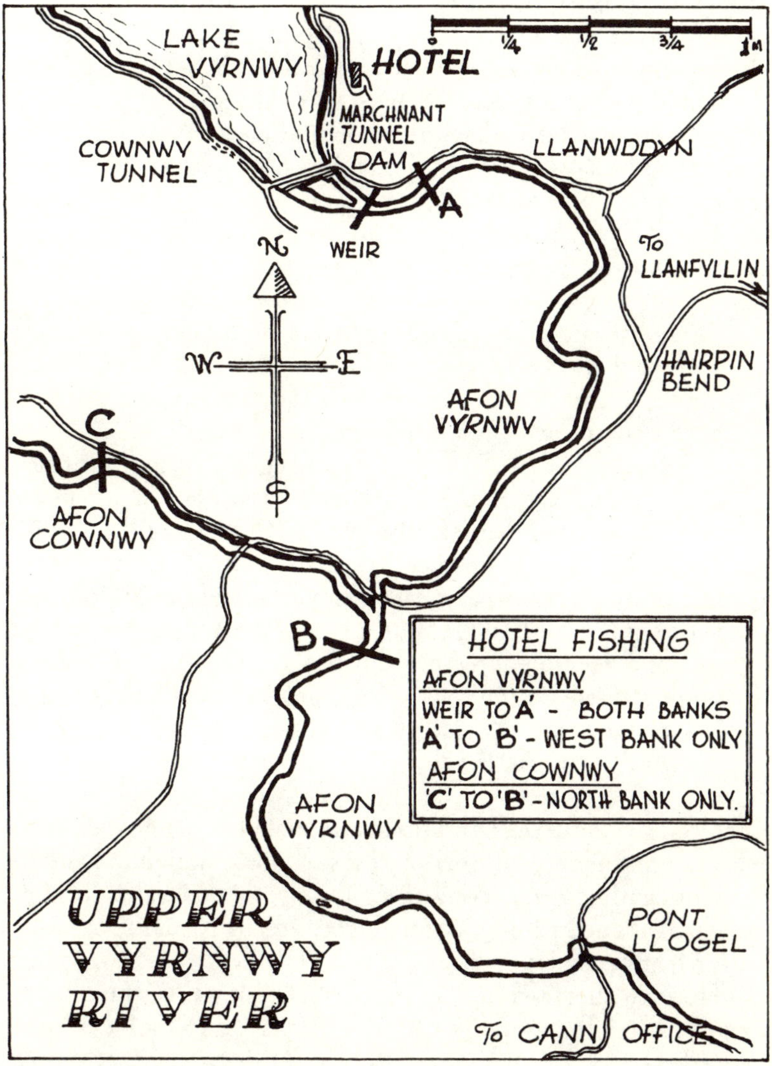
LAKE VYRNWY
HOTEL
0 1/4 1/2 3/4 1M
MARCHNANT TUNNEL
DAM
COWNWY TUNNEL
LLANWDDYN
A
WEIR
N
To LLANFYLLIN
W
E
S
HAIRPIN BEND
AFON VYRNWY
C
AFON COWNWY
B
HOTEL FISHING
AFON VYRNWY
WEIR TO 'A' - BOTH BANKS
'A' TO 'B' - WEST BANK ONLY
AFON COWNWY
'C' TO 'B' - NORTH BANK ONLY.
AFON VYRNWY
UPPER VYRNWY RIVER
PONT LLOGEL
To CANN OFFICE

full for much of the year. The breathtaking experience of millions of gallons of water shooting over the dam during the winter months, which helped clean out the river and carried many trout with it, is now rare.

The river was once a little gem. Ronnie Carpenter tells of many expeditions when he was a lad with his father Sim when a basket of 20 fish was the rule rather than the exception. Richard Threlfall was an aficionado of the river which, as he says in his 1947 book, he knew 'indecently well, practically stone by stone'.

Threlfall gives some useful advice to the first time river fisher on the Vyrnwy: He says:

'In up-stream wet-fly fishing throw no longer a line than you need and be most careful to see that it is never slack. Short, quick casts, never two in the same place, are far better than fewer and longer ones.

The tails of pools do not usually get all the attention they should. Often the fishermans' approach to them is very obvious; more often the increasing speed of the water causes his dry-fly to drag outrageously. Drag does not normally carry in the Vyrnwy the penalties that it does in, for example, the Itchin, but it should be avoided as much as possible except when you are fishing broken rocky water. The best day for fishing pool tails is when a strong up-stream wind is blowing and you can get close to, and almost dap at, the fish.'

Seldom reaching the half pound mark, seven to nine inch fish are caught in large numbers by those skilled enough to handle the difficult casting conditions facing the fisherman. The steep banks and proliferation of trees and brush make casting a far from easy business.

Here, waders are a necessity. Make sure that they have studded or felt soles since the rocks and boulders are treacherous to say the least with weed slime. Never attempt wading in the rubber soled variety as this will probably result in a cold ducking or worse.

Owing to the problems already mentioned, a rod of 8 feet is admirably suited for the job. Anything longer will mean trouble with overhanging branches. The river is narrow over the great part of the Hotel's beat and long casting is not required. In fact it is easy to get hung up on the trees on the far bank.

A sharp tweak of the rod usually frees the fly but, failing this, put down the rod and 'hand-line'. Since you are bound to get caught up in a situation like this at least once during an expedition, always have a spare made-up cast or two in the fishing bag for a quick change-over. I suggest 4 lb or 6 lb breaking strain nylon and the cast should be no longer than your rod.

The trout are apt to lie under trees overhanging the river. Experience of what I like to call 'sideways' casting – casting with the rod parallel to the water – is invaluable. The hard-to-master 'Spey' cast can come in useful as well.

When approaching a pool, always fish from the tail and never start at the head. The fish are facing upstream on the look out for food and will spot you immediately. They dash for cover long before you have a chance to cover them.

Caution is the watchword. Cast upstream if possible, look out for potholes, and keep out of sight whenever approaching the pool or run you intend fishing.

There is no doubt that the dry fly affords more amusement on the river than fishing 'wet'. For those preferring to fish 'wet', it is worth remembering to use large brightly hued flies when there is a considerable volume of coffee coloured water pouring down the river. In quieter conditions, use smaller flies in the 14 and 16 size range.

It will prove a useful exercise yet again to ask which patterns are attracting fish at the moment.

The dry fly enthusiast should tie darker patterns to fly on to the end of the cast. Colours recommended by Richard Threlfall are 'reddish, dark blue or black'.

It is to be hoped that the problem with the waterflow into the Hotel beat on the River can be overcome during the next year or so. This is a matter for Severn-Trent Water.

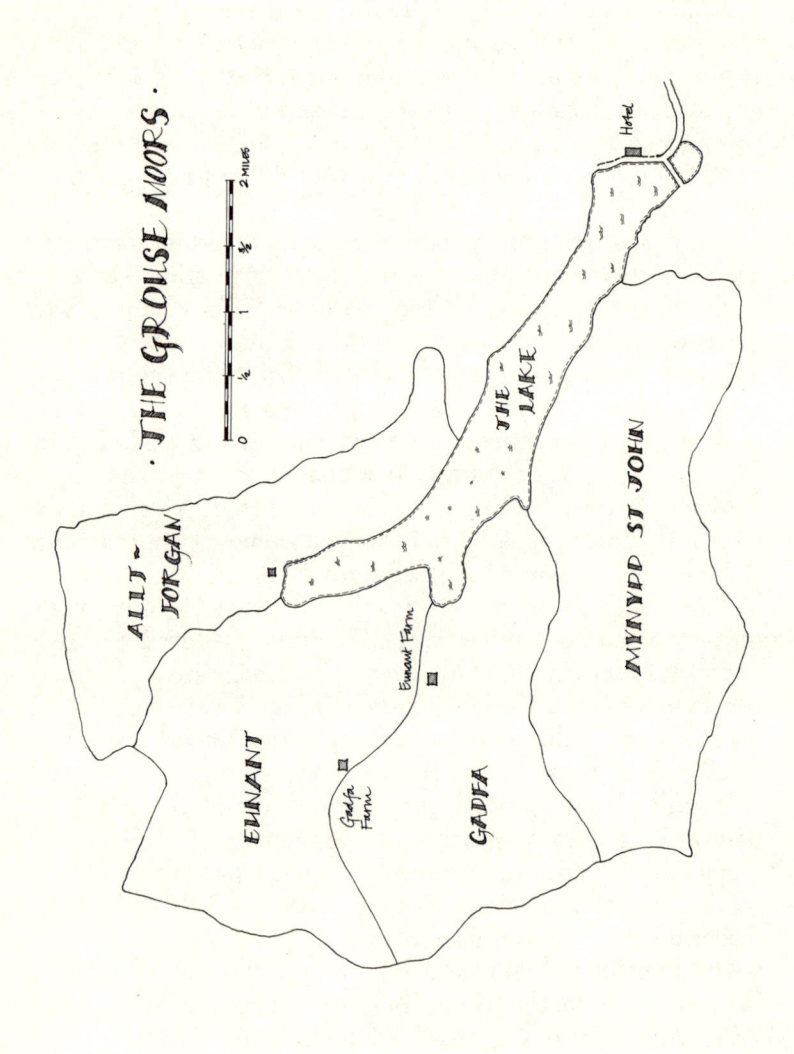

# CHAPTER EIGHT

# The Shooting Rights

*1890–1914*

Having purchased the extensive estate surrounding the new reservoir, the Liverpool Corporation had to consider how to take advantage of its sporting potential. As well as establishing the fishery, measures were put in hand to let the shooting rights to a suitable tenant. Given the relative inaccessability of Lake Vyrnwy in those days, people coming to shoot were bound to require accommodation, and so it was natural to involve the hotel in the shooting scene, as well as the fishing, from the start.

As explained earlier, the estate was gradually built up to cover 24,000 acres, and eventually to 26,000. From the sporting angle it was divided into two parts: the grouse moors, forming a rough horse-shoe around the northern end of the lake, and the low-ground shooting. On the south west side, on the moor known as Mynydd St John, the Earl of Powis retained the shooting rights, as did Sir Watkin Williams-Wynn over the land he had sold on the eastern side.

While the lessees of the hotel appear to have been given first refusal over renting the grouse moors, the lease of them was kept separate from that of the low-ground shooting, as could be seen in the wording of the advertisement quoted in Chapter 4. Although no lessee did ever refuse to take the moors, there was the opportunity to do so. Needless to say, they were a valuable asset to the business, as the hotel needed every bit of 'drawing-power' to bring customers to its isolated situation.

An idea of what was available to a guest around 1908 can be seen in this extract from W. M. Gallichan's book *Lake Vyrnwy and Around*, already referred to by George Westropp:

## 'SHOOTING'

'The tract of country within the shooting rights of the Hotel covers about 40,000 acres. The greater part of the preserve consists of grouse moors, of which there are four, each one extensive and well stocked. Grouse thrive on the Berwyn Mountains, the high situation and the vegetation, especially the great acreage of heather, being extremely favourable for their increase. No better grouse moors can be found in Wales, nor even in the Kingdom, than those heath-covered uplands between Llangollen and Lake Vyrnwy. The country is well adapted for walking up the birds with dogs or for driving the grouse.

Close to the Hotel is a big moor, reserved for shooting visitors. Grouse may be put up within a few hundred yards of the house, and there are plenty of rabbits and a few hares on this beat. The total bag of grouse for the season of 1908 was 800 brace.

The many coverts on both sides of the Lake harbour a large number of pheasants, and intersting shooting may be enjoyed in the coppices at the further end of the water, and in the numerous plantations and hanging woods on the estate. Rabbits breed in large numbers almost everywhere up to a height of about 1,000 feet, and they are especially abundant around the Lake where the herbage is green and sweet.

Woodcock are frequently shot around Lake Vyrnwy. Snipe, both common and jack-snipe, visit all the morasses, marshes and pools of the district. Here and there the gunner will meet with coveys of partridges in the low-lying parts of the preserve. Blackcock are not common in any part of Wales, but there are a few in the neighbourhood of Llanwddyn.

The gunner will vary his bag with an occasional wood-pigeon or plover. Curlews breed on the Berwyns, and visit the range in considerable flocks. Golden plovers are visitors to the moors, and breed on the Berwyns.

Hard weather brings a varied company of wildfowl to the Lake and the district around. Geese are often seen on the water, and wild swans are visitors. Ducks of several species resort to the sheet of water, and flocks may be seen almost every day, while there are regular nesting places on the islets and around the shores. Sheldrakes sometimes appear on the Lake, teal, widgeon and mallards also visit the locality.'

The figure of 40,000 acres is accounted for by the fact that the hotel rented extra moorland from Sir Watkin Williams-Wynn, and a lot of low-ground shooting on farms in the direction of Llanfyllin, in addition to the rights taken from the Lake Vyrnwy estate.

The four moors mentioned are the three main ones known as Gadfa, Eunant, and Allt-Forgan, plus the moor immediately north of the hotel, which to-day is barely recognisable as such. Grass has now replaced most of the heather, and a large area is covered by forestry. Grouse have not been seen there for 20 years.

While the moor near the hotel was, as Gallichan reports, 'reserved for shooting visitors', the three main ones were sub-let to either syndicates, or individuals, depending on circumstances. Naturally those who took the grouse shooting were expected to stay in the hotel. Mr G. G. Barker rented Allt-Forgan moor for some years at the turn of the century, and brought his party of friends and relations to stay at the hotel. In recent years his son, Brigadier C. N. Barker has been able to recognise some of the places shown in his father's old photo-albums while fishing at the northern end of the lake below Allt-Forgan mountain.

Up to 1914 the total number of grouse shot each year averaged 800 brace or more. During the war this average fell to less than half, the total for 1917 being 355 brace. The reasons were set out very clearly in a letter from William Hampson to Lieutenant-Colonel J. R. Davidson, DSO, the Liverpool Corporation water engineer, on 4 September 1918. This was one of several letters, already referred to in an earlier chapter, which were written at the time in connection with the search for someone to take over the hotel when Hampson's lease expired in 1919. Mr Caley, negotiating on behalf of the syndicate which eventually did take over, had clearly been running down the moors in hopes of lowering the rent:

As regards the moors, they [the syndicate] seem to think because the present tenant has made such small bags, the moors will never realise the pre-War rents. Mr Docker has taken the moors at much less than half the pre-War rent, £300 as against £680, and he knew quite well it has been impossible to do the usual keepering. Up to 1914 I had four keepers, three of them joined the Army as volunteers and one has been killed in action in France.

I can give you very good reasons why the present tenant's bags have been so small, and I am assured by my keeper there is a very good stock of birds in the moors at the present time. But if the war lasts much longer I am afraid serious damage will be done to the moors by vermin – for so many keepers are killing vermin in another form in France.'

The one keeper left was Tom Hughes, who spent most of his working life on the Vyrnwy estate, from about 1892 up to 1937.

During the war two measures were put in hand which were not helpful for the long-term grouse prospects on the moors: the numbers of sheep were increased as part of the war-effort, and a programme of planting more trees around the edge of the moorland areas was started.

A certain number of pheasants were reared on the low-ground each year up to the war, but never on the scale that was to become the practice in later years.

*1919–1947*

In 1919 William Hampson retired, and the syndicate comprising Messrs Caley and James and Major J. G. Lowndes took over the lease of the hotel, as has already been described.

About two years after the change over, Major Lowndes, the most active member of the syndicate, became incensed at the loss of lambs on the farm due to the depradations of foxes. He therefore started a small pack of hounds, which were kennelled in a wooden shed in the hotel grounds. It was a foot pack, supported by men with guns, who were placed at strategic points round woods and coverts in order to shoot any foxes which were pushed out by the hounds. A worker on the estate wrote a poem about a hunting day, describing Major Lowndes, who always rode to the meets. Written first in Welsh, it was put into English by the school-master in Llanwddyn:

The day for hunting Reynard
Wakes up the countryside,
When the Major to the hunting field
With Vyrnwy's pack doth ride.

He's off to mount Ty-Uchaf
With shouts of 'Tally-ho',
And he's humming at the canter
'A hunting we will go'.

Hark! Listen to the horn
And answer to its call,
For Mr Hill is shouting
'On guard!' you gunners all.

And now the hounds are prowling
In forest, field, and fen,
Intent to find old Reynard
And drive him from his den

The Corporation workers
Think of the day with joy,
And wonder in the morning
Who'll be the lucky boy.

The lucky one at watch
Concealed behind a bush,
Who'll shoot the cunning creature
And carry home his brush.

Mr Hill, the farm baliff also rode to the meet, accompanied by his daughter Ruby, who held the three horses while hunting was in progress.

The shooting during the inter-war years was conducted on similar lines to that established before 1914, but the emphasis altered as the bags of grouse shot on the moors never recovered to the average figures expected earlier. The result was that the low-ground shooting was given more attention, and the numbers of pheasants reared was steadily increased. In addition to the reared pheasant shoot, often let to a syndicate, there was an extensive rough shoot, kept for small parties of guns, or individuals, staying in the hotel.

In a book entitled *Shooting Ways and Shooting Days*, J. C. M. Nichols produced an account of how the rough shoot was operated in the 1920s:

'Quite the best shooting hotel I have stayed at is the well-known Lake Vyrnwy Hotel in North Wales, at which I made a short stay in October, 1929. They do you well; and anyone who is not afraid of hard work, i.e. walking hills which could well be called mountains, and content with a modest bag of say six to ten head of wild grouse or equally wild pheasants, might find much to please him at Vyrnwy.

The hotel shootings ran to (I believe) some 20,000 acres of moors and woodlands for the accommodation of shooting guests. There was also an extensive acreage of "driving" moor which was usually let by the season.

Our usual procedure (two guns) was to go out with a keeper who, with his retriever and two spaniels, would work the higher moorland; sometimes posting the guns forward, or again himself taking the crest of the hills, with the guns walking a flank along some tiny goat-path or as best they could. Every now and again a grouse or outlying pheasant would be flushed, to come rocketing out across the valley, and giving perchance a wonderful high curling shot to one or other of the guns. The shooting was rendered doubly difficult as quite probably one would be caught negotiating an extra steep bit, with one foot a yard higher than the other.

Should I revist Vyrnwy, I think my age and dignity would require the services of one of those sturdy little Welsh shooting-ponies, of which the hotel stables held some half-dozen or more. There were a few partridges to be found on the lower ground, and on the hills we generally flushed two or three black-cock. We were told that these fine birds were much scarcer than they had been a few years previously.

Talking of Vyrnwy reminds me of one of the best retrieves I have ever seen. Towards the end of a long day's tramp, a pheasant had been just wing-tipped and dropped into some of the roughest undergrowth, a very lively runner. Jones, the keeper, was engaged in beating; and his dog, a black labrador, could not be given the line till some minutes afterwards.

We sat down to smoke a pipe and give the dog time to work, and finally as dusk was falling, prepared to start on our homewards walk. I then caught sight of a black dot coming towards us from a tremendous distance over the hill. "Here's your dog at last," I said, "and he will have your bird, moreover," answered Jones in quiet triumph.'

In March 1930 a new head-keeper, William Robert Bull, arrived from Ireland to take charge of the pheasant shoot. Soon afterwards, in May, he was joined by his 23 year-old son, also William, who still lives in Llanwddyn and has provided much interesting information about the way things were done in those days. As well as the two Bulls, there was a third keeper, who also looked after the fox-hounds which were still kept at the hotel.

Rearing pheasants was harder work than it has become in more recent years. Eggs were hatched under broody hens, which were put out into a rearing field in wooden coops. Each hen looked after 15 foster chicks. The coops were set out at 25 yard intervals, the lines of them stretching up the hill towards Ty-Llwyd farm from the bottom of the quarry valley. At six weeks the coops, complete with hen and poults, as the chicks had now become, were taken to be put out in the woods. The hens stayed with their broods until late August or September. After a short time out in the woods the coops were put up onto wooden stands about five feet high, which meant that the poults had to lean to fly up the roost in the evenings, an important lesson in the process of learning to survive in the wild.

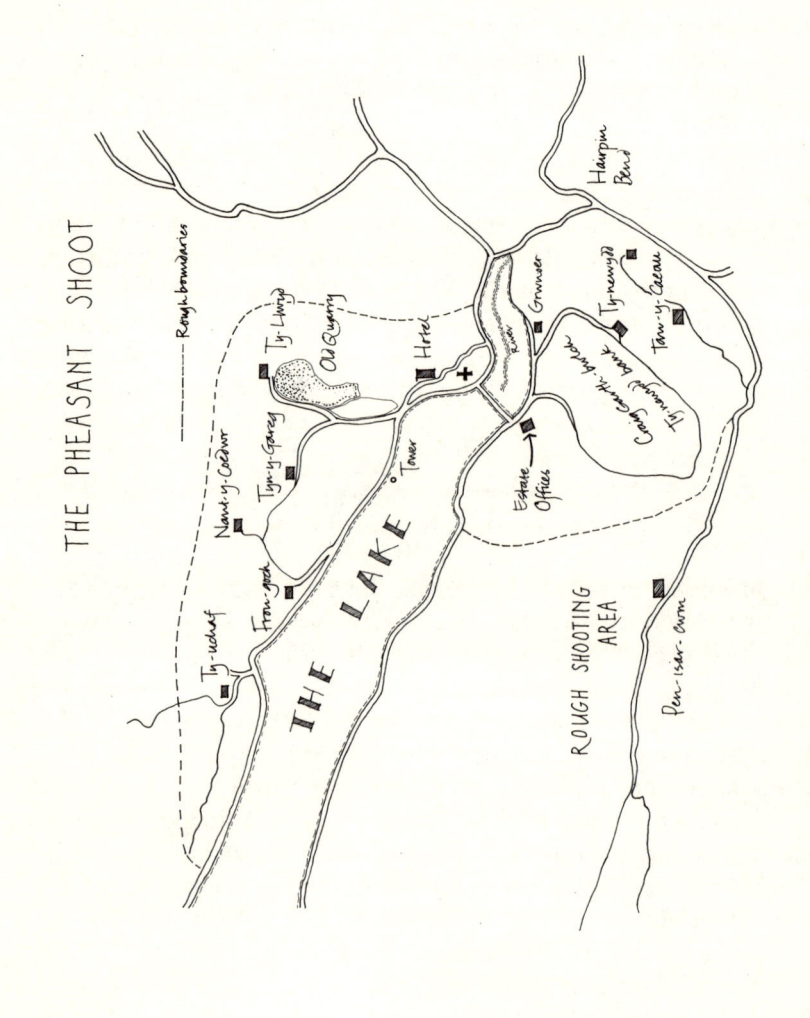

The preparation of food for the young pheasants was a laborious and time consuming job. The chicks were started on hard boiled eggs pushed through a seive. Later they moved onto boiled meat of various sorts mixed with game meal. The big boiler in which all the food was prepared was in a shed at the bottom of the quarry valley. Finally the well-grown young birds were introduced to their basic diet, wheat.

During the 1930s the driven pheasant shoot was taken by a syndicate from Birmingham. Graham Martin had a gun in it, in return for his supervision of the shoot, and organisation of the shooting days. The party came up every fortnight and shot on two days, either a Friday and Saturday, or a Saturday and the following Monday. Officially 2,000 pheasants were reared, but William Bull reckons that his father contrived to make the figure nearer 2,500. The best season he remembers was 1934, when the total bag was 1,912 – a remarkable return considering the numbers released. On 23 November that year Graham Martin's game-book shows the record score of 412. Then, as now, the shoot was renowed for some spectacular high drives. In the description of the Vyrnwy river, in his book *Wanderings with a Fly-rod*, Sir Edward Durand breaks off from the subject of fishing for to include this paragraph, which starts with mention of a bridge no longer to be found:

'This iron cart-bridge lies just below the covert-clad hill-top which is called "Garrison Wood", one of the finest stands for high pheasants it has ever been my pleasure to watch. On the first occasion I saw it driven over the guns, standing in the meadows between it and the river, not one bird of all that came over could have been called an easy shot. I envied each gun in turn as I watched a succession of cocks, looking the size of starlings with long tails, sailing out into the clear air and making for the young plantation on the opposite hill-side, over the river and road.'

In 1934 William Bull was transferred from the pheasant shoot to the moors, where he became assistant to Tom Hughes. Outside the shooting season the moorland keepers' main duty was to wage a constant war on vermin, especially foxes and crows. Whenever the weather was suitable during the months when it was legally permissible they worked hard to burn as much heather as possible. As the start of the shooting season approached time was spent repairing existing butts and building new ones.

Gadfa moor was reserved for walking-up, as was what was left, after afforestation, of the moor just above the hotel. Eunant and Allt-Forgan were the main driving moors. The totals of grouse shot each year at this time can be seen at Appexdix B. Some idea of the bags on individual days can be given by reference to two sources: the personal game-book of Graham Martin, recently rediscovered in South Africa by his son, and some notes provided by Mr Michael Barker, who was a member of the syndicate which took the driven grouse shooting at Vyrnwy for most of the 1930s.

A few random entries from Graham's game-book give an impression of the sport provided.

*August 17, 1932*: 9 guns on Allt-Forgan shot 43½ brace.
   Comment: 'Gorgeous day and shot well.'
*October 28, 1933*: 8 guns on Allt-Forgan shot 21 brace.
   Comment: 'Devilish cold and unpleasant.'
*September 1, 1934*: 8 guns on Gadfa and Eunant shot 20½ brace.
   Comment: 'Fine with a few heavy showers. Gadfa better than usual. Shooting poor.'
*August 15, 1936*: 8 guns on Allt-Forgan shot 57½ brace.
   Comment: 'In the clouds in the morning, which was spoilt. Improving in afternoon. Wind in west.'

Michael Barker's notes from three years in the 1930s show what the syndicate achieved. In 1935 they had six days' shooting and shot a total of 242 brace, with a best day of 54½ brace. In 1937 seven days yielded 277 brace, with a best day of 76. The outbreak of war had a disastrous effect on the results for 1939, with only five days and a total bag of 131½ brace, the best day being 36 brace on Allt-Forgan on 16 August.

Comparing the syndicate's results with the full total of grouse shot in these years shows that the walking moors must have added considerably to each season's bag. For example, in 1937 there were an additional 130 brace shot over and above those killed on the driving days.

Some of the ponies kept at the hotel had a part to play on the moors. One followed the guns with two panniers slung over its back to carry the game, while another, similarly equipped, brought out the lunch each day. On Allt-Forgan moor there was a wooden lunch hut for use at the Bala end. Ponies were also made available for any guns unable to walk up to their butts to ride to them. The manpower required to provide all the necessary beaters, flankers, pony men and pickers-up was provided partly by the permanent gamekeepers, but also by up to 20 more Corporation men working on the estate. It was possible for the hotel to have ready call on this source of labour, under an arrangment worked out with Humphrey Howard, for the pheasant shoot as well as for the grouse moors.

On 12 August each year the opening of the season was celebrated by a special dinner in the hotel, the menu for which relied to a great extent on home produced items:

Vyrnwy soup – usually game
Vyrnwy trout – caught in the lake
Vyrnwy grouse – young birds brought down at lunch time from the moors
Vyrnwy strawberries and cream – strawberries grown in the garden
Vyrnwy savoury – a kind of pâté on wafers

A good picture of how the whole range of the hotel's shooting facilties were organized between the wars can be found in a full page advertisement placed in *Game and Gun* magazine in November 1935. It takes the form of an imaginary letter from a certain Dick, who is writing to his friend Charles, shortly due to return to Britain for a long leave from some outpost of the Empire:

Dear Charles,
I understand you are coming home on leave in November, and that you are anxious to obtain some shooting. I gather that you do not wish to go to the expense of taking your own shoot, with all its ties and responsibilities. A syndicate shoot would probably not appeal to you, with its

pre-arranged dates and a fixed sum down. Have you thought of some of the best known sporting hotels?

I stayed last year at the Lake Vyrnwy Hotel, just over the Welsh border, in the Montgomeryshire mountains. This hotel has the shooting over 21,000 acres of wonderful sporting country, and six keepers are employed.

During November and December you can get some first-class rough shooting walking up for 25/- a day. Last year we had some excellent bags up to 25 head, wild pheasants were the principal item, also we got a few grouse, blackgame, hill partridges, mallard, rabbits, etc. These pheasants, being so often flushed off a steep hillside, give most sporting shots. Some 2,000 pheasants are reared annually for a syndicate run by the hotel (which I gather is fully booked for this year). Naturally some of these birds have spread out over a number of years and have built up a fine head of wild stock. Shooting parties are arranged every other day and are limited to four guns to a party. There are rabbits and pigeons to shoot on odd days, for which there is no charge.

Covert shooting is available to experienced guns on pre-arranged dates; the bags are not large, probably 30 to 40 pheasants, but very high birds are the order of the day. The cost of this is £3 to £4 a day.

The shooting continues throughout January, but is limited to cock pheasants only, which will cost you 10/- a day, and the circumvention of some of those wily old cocks is no mean feat.

If you are in England earlier another year they can provide you with some good grouse shooting. During August and September there is driving over two moors, where the bags run from 40 to 60 brace on the best moor, and 20 to 30 brace on the smaller moor, prices £4 to £7 a day. This may sound a lot of money, but you must remember that in this country grouse rents are about £1 a brace, and what with beaters' wages, etc., I cannot see how they can do it any cheaper.

Last year I went out on two other moors which they keep for walking up, and our party had bags up to 10 brace of grouse and a few blackgame. For this we were charged

25/- a day. It was all very enjoyable.

As for the hotel, it is a nice, warm country house, really well run, and in the winter terms are very moderate. They also have ponies and cobs for riding.

In the spring and summer you would have to go far afield to find better rainbow and brown trout fishing.

I suggest you write direct to the hotel.

Yrs.,
Dick.

When war came in 1939 shooting was soon restricted to hunting for the pot. The days of driven grouse and reared pheasants were soon forgotten. William Bull switched from keepering to full-time employment with the Corporation, and the other keepers were diverted to work more productive for the war-effort. The few people who continued to go out from time to time with a gun were either too old to have war-time duties, or were officers taking short periods of leave at the hotel. Such game as they brought back with them was much appreciated in the kitchens.

With the departure of all the keepers, vermin soon established a hold on the countryside. Foxes and crows proliferated, and gradually reduced the grouse stocks almost to vanishing point. Only a few old cock pheasants survived on the lower ground. Because of the depradations of foxes, as well as trapping and occasional shooting by man, even the rabbits were unable to breed successfully enough for their numbers to be maintained at pre-war level.

After the end of the war in 1945, a keeper was once more employed by the hotel. The first man in the job, named Lloyd, devoted most of his time to killing foxes and trapping rabbits. William Bull remained on the strength of the Liverpool Corporation, but was released at times to help with the fox clearance programme. This was much encouraged throughout the country by a scheme whereby 10/- was paid for every brush of a fox brought in to certain designated places. In days when, for example, the pay of a recruit for the armed forces was 3/- a day, it can be seen that 10/- was rather more valuable than it might at first appear.

## 1947–1972

When the Moirs took over the hotel on 8 March 1947, the sporting part of their lease only covered the low-ground shooting rights. At the instigation of Humphrey Howard, the resident agent, it included among other conditions a limit of 500 on the number of pheasants that could be reared each season. This was to avoid excessive damage to the arable crops which were still grown on farms on the estate for feeding stock in the winter, a practice which continued for some years after the war. The grouse moors were let to the hotel on a different basis, which entailed an annual agreement at an agreed price. Though the hotel was given first chance to bid for the moors each year, they could have been let to other people if satisfactory agreement had not been reached. This eventuality in fact never arose.

Opening a new game book in 1947, Jamie Moir wrote in it as follows:

'On taking over Lake Vyrnwy Hotel on 8 March 1947 the amount of game on the shootings was negligible, rabbits and wild pheasants having been practically exterminated, but vermin, particularly foxes were present in considerable numbers. It will be of interest to see from this record whether the shooting will be brought back, and how long it will take.'

To augment the hotel's own shooting, where Lloyd the keeper continued to direct most of his energies to fox control, Jamie Moir took the shooting rights on several farms lying to the south-east of the lake, along the road to Llanfyllin. Well on into the 1950s all these farms had extensive areas of ground under cultivation for corn and root crops, and partridges were plentiful. Two of them Cewnant and Cammen Fawr, are shown in the game book to have provided some pleasant, mixed rough shooting in 1954. The season's bag on these two farms comprised 48 partridges, 30 pheasants, 24 snipe, 1 duck, 25 wood pigeons, 2 hares, and 66 rabbits, mostly shot by Jamie Moir on his own, out for an afternoon with his dogs. On occasions he would be accompanied by one or two guests from the hotel, or personal friends.

While continuing to rent this shooting on the road to Llanfyllin, and also some other ground to the west of the lake up the Cownwy valley, Jamie was improving conditions on the hotel's own shooting, and on the moors. He was putting down 100 pheasants by this time in the neighbourhood of the hotel, while the fox killing programme was giving the grouse a chance to recover on the moors. By 1958 there is no mention of Cewnant and Cammen Fawr farms in the game book, the total bag for the season being almost entirely shot within the hotel's own rights. It amounted to 129 grouse, 72 pheasants, 2 woodcock, 3 snipe, 5 duck, 8 wood pidgeon, and 5 hares. The arrival of myxamatosis had by then removed all the rabbits, of which 229 had been killed only two years previously.

Throughout his time at the hotel Jamie kept yellow labradors, and bred some very good dogs which he trained to a high standard. During the winter in the 1950s, when the hotel was quiet, he went for a walk in the afternoon, with a gun and his dogs, several times a week. For example, in January 1957 the game book shows that he was out on eleven days, nine times on his own, and twice with one other person. Later, during the 1960s, his name appears less regularly, while there are more mentions of hotel guests shooting. During this decade the grouse were making something of a comeback, as can be seen in the figures at Appendix B. Bags of over ten brace a day, by six guns walking-up, began to be recorded in the game book. On 12 August 1970 a party of six shot 22 brace at the Cedig end of Allt-Forgan moor, the best single day's bag since 1939, and unlikely ever to be improved upon again.

*1972-1992*

During the week-end marking the retirement of Jamie Moir and the arrival of myself and my family, which was described in Chapter 5, one of the activities laid on was a short day's grouse driving on Eunant moor on 28th October 1972. Although limitations on time available only allowed for three drives, a good number of birds were seen, and 12½ brace were shot. All arrangements for the day depended on William Bull, who had previously given me a guided tour of all the moors, and shown me all the old lines of butts, and the ways to reach them. On this day he had collected a good team of beaters, and directed them with skill, making full use of all the knowledge he had absorbed as a young moor keeper well over 30 years previously. The season's bag of grouse for 1972 was 88½ brace.

The following year our shooting efforts were again concentrated on the moors, with only 100 pheasants turned into covert. In the game book I wrote some notes on the 1973/74 season, during which the number of grouse shot was 111½ brace, the highest total from 1939 until to-day, and alas likely to remain so. My notes read as follows:

'The grouse season opened with a period of hot sunny weather, which lasted well into the second week. The stock of birds was about average, with quite a number of cheepers seen. These must have been second broods following some unusually heavy thunderstorms in late May at the time of hatching, which must have caused a certain amount of damage.

A feature of August was the number of hen harriers seen over the moors, particularly to the north-east of the lake over Allt-Forgan. The tendency was for the grouse to be driven away from the tops to the fringes of the moors. How much the stock of grouse was actually depleted by the harriers is hard to know, but they were certainly moved from some of the areas where they were expected to be found.

As apparently often happens in this part of Wales, the grouse seemed to be more plentiful as the season progressed. But this may well have been merely due to a lot of birds having sat very tight early on in the hot weather, and only showing themselves later in the season.

A driving day was held on Allt-Forgan on 6 October. A lot of birds were seen, though they were strong, wild, and far from easy to shoot!'

Special mention was accorded to 6 October because on all the other 20 days that year that parties went out they walked up the birds, and it was the only time driving was attempted. During the following four seasons more frequent driving days were organised but were not often very successful. 11 brace on Gadfa on 21 September 1974 was one of the better bags achieved. All too often remarks in the game book include comments such as 'fiendish weather – gales and rain', or 'strong wind and very wet'. As an alternative, the weather was recorded on 14 November 1975 as fine with an east wind, but the small bag on Allt-Forgan was put down to a different reason! 'A good show of birds on the last two drives, but marksmanship not as good as it might have been.'

As can be seen from a glance at the figures in Appendix B, the totals of grouse shot each year held up reasonably well until 1977. At the end of that season I wrote in the game book that: 'The grouse were a puzzle in 1977. At the beginning of the season there did not seem to be many about, but by the end of September there were quite a lot.' I went on to explain that the decision had been made to cut down the amount of walking-up in August, and then recorded the story of a driving day rained off on 24 September. However my notes ended confidently:

> 'The next week on Gadfa wind and rain, and sometimes hail, came as well. But the stock of birds was remarkable, and on the first drive we saw a great many. Several coveys broke back, but even so we got four brace at that one drive, all coming like rockets.
>
> On 8 October we had a very good day. We could only manage four drives, as cloud on the hill delayed our start. Again, the birds were hard to hit, and the total bag of 13 brace does not really indicate the very healthy numbers seen.'

The following year, 1978, saw the start in the downturn in the grouse stock which has never picked up again during the succeeding years. At the end of the entries in the game book this note was inserted:

'The 1978 grouse season can only be described as disastrous. The total bag was only 46½ brace, and we shot far too many old birds in this number compared to young ones.

Where the grouse have disappeared to is a mystery, as both Gadfa and Eunant moors carried very good stocks at the end of 1977. However, all moors around the Vyrnwy area seem to be in the same state.

It remains to be seen whether we can allow any shooting at all on the moors in 1979. If the early walking-up days in August show that there is a serious shortage of birds we will have to cancel the later days.'

During 1979 and 1980 Eunant continued to produce some quite good days, but little could be found on Gadfa and Allt-Forgan, both of which moors were only visited once. Throughout the 1980s the pattern remained the same, though occasionally signs of recovery in certain places made us think that an upturn in numbers might be underway. For example, on 31 August 1985 a day with two drives on Gadfa and two on Eunant produced 12½ brace, with enough birds seen to have shot 20 brace with better marksmanship. Those two moors were left alone apart from that one day, but in spite of this there was once again a shortage in 1986. Since then we have shot the three moors more and more lightly, but it has made little difference: the steady decline in numbers has gone on inexorably.

It was an attempt to find ways of combating this steady decrease in our stock that a seminar was held in the hotel on 25 March 1982 to discuss 'The Decline of Red Grouse in Wales'. The late Sir Watkin Williams-Wynn was in the chair, and experts who came to speak included Lord Peel and Dr Peter Hudson from the North of England Grouse Research Project; Frank Best, owner of Vivod moor; John Anderton of BASC; Roger Lovegrove of the RSPB; and John Phillips, well known as an independent game adviser. A large number of moor owners and tenants, syndicate members, and game keepers attended, as well as what might be termed occasional grouse shooters. In all, nearly 90 people crowded into the big drawing-room in the hotel. The proceedings were extensively written up in *The Field* by Dick Orton, and in *The Shooting Times* by John Buckland. I made a brief summary of the day's findings, from which the following paragraphs have been extracted:

'Grouse have declined in numbers in Wales since a peak in 1915. This was to be expected during the two World Wars, and after each a revival took place, though figures never again came near the 1915 level. The big worry is that the revival from 1950 to 1975 has not been sustained, and from 1978 onwards nearly all Welsh moors have shown a steady downward trend.

The three causes of this decline are common to other parts of the country, but their effect in Wales is more pronounced than elsewhere due to the poor grouse habitat provided by most of the hill land. High rainfall, poor quality shale sub-soil, and consequently slow re-generating and easily destroyed heather have always made the grouse population in Wales smaller than that found in the North of England and much of Scotland.

The three main causes themselves are the spread of forestry, excessive grazing by sheep often accompanied by careless farming methods, and the attacks of ever-increasing number of vermin, especially foxes and crows. When these harmful factors are all found together grouse are in danger of extinction. The smaller the stock of birds on a moor the greater the danger becomes.

The only way to restore the situation is by good management. This entails systematic, well-organised heather burning, control of sheep stocks, and good keepering. Given the will and the resources to manage a moor well, there is no reason why one in Wales should not hold a sufficient head of grouse to provide reasonable sport, in spite of the fact that the habitat is not good enough to sustain stocks such as are known in other parts of Britain.

Unfortunately, on many Welsh moors the situation may have been reached where the will and the resources to restore the grouse are lacking. There are too few game-keepers, and those that there are usually spend most of their energies looking after pheasants. Furthermore, when grouse have become scarce, it takes a long time to build them up again, and there is no return in the short-term for the time and money which has to be devoted to the necessary work. But unless something is done it is more than likely that eventually grouse in Wales will become extinct.

Above all, we must actually DO something to put matters right. There is no point in talking endlessly about the problems unless action is taken to solve them. It is sincerely hoped that everyone who can help in any way will make the effort to stop the steady decline of the grouse in Wales towards its all too possible extinction.'

Although everyone departed full of resolve to DO something, Shakespeare's words from *The Merchant of Venice* came to mind: 'If to do were as easy as to know what were good to do, chapels had been churches, and poor men's cottages princes' palaces.' As John Buckland pointed out in his article, 'management is expensive, clearly very expensive if conducted ideally', and this factor above all others is the one that has prevented a full-scale effort to restore the grouse population in Wales.

In the years where it has been possible, due to dryer than normal weather, we have worked hard at Vyrnwy to burn as much heather as can be tackled within the legal time limits. However, due to the extent of the moors, the proportion burnt is relatively small. As far as vermin control is concerned, the main effort has been directed towards keeping down the number of foxes, both through the activities of the local fox-hounds and by killing cubs in the summer. Crows are less easy to deal with, and are present in greater numbers than desirable. To do much more than is done already would mean a massive injection of money and labour over a period of years, at the end of which there would be no guarantee that grouse stocks would be noticeably greater. It would be a bigger gamble than anyone is likely to take.

Sadly, the prospects for grouse in Wales in the 1990s are not too good. On the three days small parties went out on the Vyrnwy moors in 1991 very few birds were seen. Reports from other places were depressingly similar. In spite of the uninspiring prospects for the future, we will continue to do all that we can with relatively limited resources to give the Vyrnwy grouse the best possible chance of survival.

During the period 1972 to 1992 certain changes have taken place in the arrangements for the hotel's lease of its shooting rights. Without going into a lot of tedious detail, there have been three main changes. The moors are now part of the overall sporting lease, whereas in 1972 they were taken on an annual basis; the 21 year lease of those days has been replaced by a 50 year one; and the limit on the number of pheasants put down has been raised from 500 to 8,500 each year. It must also be mentioned that the hotel has extended its sporting acreage by purchasing the outright ownership of the sporting rights of the moor known as Mynydd St John, lying on the south-west side of the lake, up the Cownwy valley. These 8,000 acres include low ground in the valley as well as the heather moorland.

The gradual build-up of the pheasant shoot at Vyrnwy began in 1974. Instead of just putting down 100 poults in the hotel grounds, as had been Jamie Moir's practice for many years, we decided to double that number and put them out on the shoot, in a release pen in a young wood near Tyn-y-gareg farm. The site was chosen in conjunction with William Bull, who was my valued adviser and part-time head keeper throughout much of the 1970s. On his advice we asked Trevor Hill, a member of the well-known local family mentioned earlier in the book, to build the pen for us. Trevor was a man of great practical skill and intelligence, as well as enormous physical strength, but few words. I gave him the Game Conservancy pamphlet describing how to build a release pen to work from, and he took it from me with a nod. When the work was finished the pen was a masterpiece, constructed exactly to the specification in the pamphlet. To help him Trevor had obtained the assistance of a forester on the estate called Brian Roberts, whose much greater involvement in the shoot will be described shortly.

As the years went by the number of pheasants released was steadily increased and more pens were built. Valuable help came from a Game Conservancy advisory visit by Christopher

Minchin. Our average return on numbers put down was over 50%: for example 207 out of 400 in 1977, and 279 out of 500 in 1979. In 1981 we were up to 1,000 released, with 473 shot. By 1985 we were up to 2,500 put down with a return of over 50% at 1,313 shot, but were nearer the national average the following season, with a total bag of only 1,156 from the same number released to covert.

As the shoot was enlarged more drives were opened up, some being ones remembered by William Bull and others from pre-1939 days, and some developed on likely looking bits of ground. Shooting took place regularly once a week, with bags eventually reaching 100 to 130 in November and early December, and 60 to 80 later in the season. Throughout these years there was no full-time keeper. When William Bull decided to reduce his involvement, Gwyn Jones took over, assisted by George Jones, recently retired from working on the estate as a blacksmith. Gwyn, known as 'Gwyn the Fox' because he ran the local hounds, was with us for three years before leaving the area, to be followed by Brian Roberts. At the time of writing Brian is of course full-time head keeper on the shoot, a position he fills with great ability, but I would like to pay tribute to all the work he did on a part-time basis before taking up his permanent post in 1987 following the sale of the hotel. In doing so Mabel, his wife must not be forgotten: the two of them devoted a large part of their free time to working with boundless enthusiasm in the building up of the shoot.

On taking over the hotel on 1 February 1987, the new owner, Mr Jim Bisiker, appointed his son Brian as sporting manager, with the major responsibility of greatly extending the amount of shooting available each season. As has already been mentioned, in another important step in this direction the sporting lease was re-negotiated with the Severn-Trent Water Authority onto a 50 year term; arrangements were made to start increasing the number of pheasants put down; and, as has just been described, Brian Roberts was taken on strength as a full-time head keeper, with two assistants.

The arrangement for the first season under new management was that I would take charge of the guns on shooting days, and Brian Bisiker would understudy me to learn his way around the various parts of the shoot. An immediate increase was made in the number of pheasants put down, with the result that the 1987/88 season's total bag was two and a half times larger than in 1986/87. Further increase the following year brought the figure up to the approximate level at which it has remained until the time of writing in 1992. In these succeeding years I have continued my involvement in the shoot, acting as assistant to Brian as well as occasional picker-up.

It would be fair to claim that the pheasant shoot at Lake Vyrnwy must now rank among the finest in the country. The quality of the birds shown is matched by the beauty of the scenery, while the comfort of the hotel adds to the pleasure of the sport. On two separate occasions at the end of a day during the 1991/92 season, a gun said to me that he had just experienced the best day's shooting he had ever known. Brian Roberts has perfected the art of showing high pheasants at their best. To watch them drifting off the hill above Ty-Llwyd farm, or rocketing out over the valley from Garrison wood, or sailing out from the Tyn-y-Gareg oaks, or indeed flying from numerous other coverts, is to see some of the finest and most testing shooting to be found anywhere in the world.

## Part IV

*Some Personal Thoughts in Hotel Keeping*

# CHAPTER NINE

## Running a Sporting Hotel

I must begin by stressing that the thoughts set down in this chapter and the one that follows it are solely the result of my 15 years at Lake Vyrnwy and the knowledge gained there, without experience of any other hotels from the management angle. Therefore anything recorded here should be regarded as applicable only to a medium-sized establishment in a rural setting, which is frequented by a sizeable proportion of visitors with an interest in the traditional field sports of hunting, shooting, and fishing. Although there is nothing particularly original in these reflections, my reason for including them in the book is that I would have found it extremely useful to have been given some notes on these lines when I plunged into the hotel business in 1972. While it would be foolish to claim that it is a trade which demands great intellectual effort to master, the main requirement for success, of constant attention to detail, needs to be backed up by a clear set of aims. In the case of a sporting establishment these are threefold: to provide good sporting facilities; to run them to the satisfaction of those who pay to enjoy them; and to provide a comfortable, well-run base from which to operate. This last point is the subject of the next chapter.

In respect of the sport they offer, there are two categories of sporting hotel. One group consists of those that have their own estates, or sporting rights under their own direct control, while the other relies on access to facilities rented from, or arranged with, neighbouring landowners. Within the first, and smaller, category, the majority are fishing pubs. Only a few are fortunate enough to have extensive sporting rights of all kinds, under their own management, on the same scale as those which Lake Vyrnwy has available.

As far as fishing is concerned, decisions have to be made on numerous matters which are roughly similar for both rivers and lakes, or lochs. Among them can be listed allocating beats or boat stations; setting prices; providing ghillies or boatmen; looking after boats; stocking policy where necessary; and control of poaching. Although 95% of fishermen and women are good sporting people, there is always the 5% to watch out for who are, in my predecessor Jamie Moir's words, both dirty and dishonest. Common sins among this small element, who cause more trouble than they are worth, include leaving boats or fishing huts untidy and full of litter; using illegal methods such as tackle to foul hook salmon rather than catch them properly, or bait on fly-only trout water; and concealing fish kept in excess of the official limit on numbers. While it is difficult to catch these sort of people, it is important to be ever watchful for them.

During my years in charge of the fishing on Lake Vrynwy I found it quite a time-consuming responsibility. People who had not previously fished the lake, or our stretch of river below the dam, had to be briefed on where to go, flies to use, likely spots to find trout, and so on. Old hands wanted to discuss the prospects for their visit, and pick up as much useful information as possible. Non-residents who came to fish had to be sold their tickets and have the local rules explained to them. Those setting out for the lake sometimes needed help with collecting equipment such as balers, rowlocks, electric outboards and batteries. It was important to check the boats at the different boat-stations regularly, in order to see that they were kept clean and in good repair. On occasions when stock fish arrived, I always accompanied the delivery lorry to check the quality and size of the trout, and to ensure they were put in at the right places around the lake. A daily duty was the entering up of the fishing register, which, after a busy day in May with large numbers of fish weighed in, could take a long time. The results recorded in the register were used to write regular reports for fishing journals. From time to time I would be informed of poachers seen on the shores of the lake, and would attempt to catch them. Usually they had disappeared, or gone into hiding in the undergrowth, by the time I arrived, but I did have an occasional success. This record of some of the tasks which came my way will give an idea of the range of just part of a fishing pub proprietor's work.

The extent of the shoot at Lake Vyrnwy, and the way it has been organised at different stages, has been described in the previous chapter. From the hotel management point of view decisions have to be made in respect of charging for the shooting; allowing access to it; booking in parties and individual guns; and disposing of the game. Based on experience, my own view is that the best way to charge for a day's driven shooting is by a set sum per brace or bird shot. Settling for an overall sum in advance, even with safeguards of additions or deductions if the actual bag differs widely from the numbers originally agreed, provides more opportunity for argument at the end of the day. Charging by the bird shot is fairer to both the provider of the sport and the customers. As long as the latter are kept informed of the numbers already shot should they care to enquire, they can have no complaint if the party shoots more than originally intended. If things go wrong, and the bag is smaller than anticipated, they at least have the satisfaction of paying less. No method is entirely satisfactory, but I am sure this is the best one. For rough shooting, or walking up grouse on a moor, the solution is different. In this case a fixed rate per day is clearly the answer, while in certain circumstances it might be wise to make no charge, but to offer the rough shooting as part of a week, or week-end, package.

A hotel running its own sporting estate must hope that all who come to shoot will stay overnight as well, and may well make this a condition of access to the sport offered. Such a rule should not be too slavishly followed if it leads to days being left unsold, and too many birds left on the ground at the end of the season. Contact should be maintained with local guns who might take January days, perhaps at special rates and without staying overnight, to fill gaps in a sticky year.

Booking in parties to shoot, and fitting in individual guns, is a time consuming business. While one season is in progress a file has to be opened to contain letters and notes of enquiries about the next, and by the time that following season has ended it will have become a bulky object. At Lake Vyrnwy most days are taken by complete parties of eight or nine guns, but there are usually one or two groups which can only muster a smaller team. When this occurs, there is an opportunity to make numbers up by putting in other small groups, or individual guns. Sometimes this works well, but occasionally the result is not too happy. Much effort is required, when these mixed days are arranged, to ensure that all goes smoothly.

Disposing satisfactorily of shot game is likely to be less of a problem for a hotel than most other shoot owners. Apart from the birds given to the guns, we use all grouse and duck shot at Lake Vyrnwy in the kitchen. For many years the majority of the pheasants have been taken away at the end of the day by a well-known local game dealer by the name of Mr Billy Roberts. Things have been made especially simple by the fact that he is also one of our most efficient and regular pickers-up. The pheasants that are not sold are available for the hotel kitchen, and their preparation for the table has been made considerably easier since an electric plucking machine was purchased in 1990.

At this point I would like to quote a passage from an article I wrote for the January 12–18, 1989 issue of *The Shooting Times*. It appeared in the first of two articles published under the heading 'The Proper Conduct of Shooting'

'Let me end with a description of what I consider a proper shooting party. The Guns are experienced Shots who love the country and take an interest in all aspects of the life of the area in which they spend the day. The ladies either shoot in the line, handle dogs, or occasionally join the beaters. Those who want only to stand and watch the Guns are quiet and observant. Each Gun kills his or her birds cleanly, and at the end of each drive has every one of them carefully marked. If by chance a bird is thought to be wounded a picker-up is carefully notified and so far as possible no move is made to the next stand until all such pricked birds are collected. Empty cartridge cases are gathered up after the drives as well. Lunch is eaten quickly and reasonably frugally, and the afternoon's shooting ends in good time for pheasants to go to roost peacefully. The beaters and pickers-up are thanked by the Guns and the headkeeper is not only given a handsome tip, but time is taken to discuss the events of the day with him knowledgeably. For such a party, the organising of a day of up to 150 well-presented birds becomes the greatest pleasure.'

So far these reflections on running a sporting hotel have been concerned with those places which possess their own fishing or shooting rights, or have full control of them under the terms of a long lease. It is now time to look briefly at the situation of the more numerous group consisting of hotels which rely entirely on rented facilities, the day-to-day management of which is not in their hands. These facilities could range from an annual lease of a stretch of river, or one or two boats on a loch, to a simple agreement with a neighbouring landowner for the occasional guest to be sent to fish his water for an agreed daily sum. A number of fishing pubs, in Scotland especially, do not even go to these lengths, but rely on their proximity to stretches of river under public ownership, where the only requirement is to have a fully paid river board licence before going down to the water.

My own limited experience of gaining access to rented fishing is concerned with two separate beats on the Welsh Dee, where in the 1970s I obtained the right for one rod at a time to fish for salmon. The conditions laid down by the owner of the first beat were justifiably strict, and included a stipulation that only hotel guests personally vetted by me should be allowed to fish it. Unfortunately, one of the guests I had sent there was later overheard boasting to a friend in a bar in Chester about the fact that he could get him salmon fishing on the Dee whenever he liked. The person listening in on the conversation was a close friend of the owner of the beat, and was easily able to recognise the location being discussed. Needless to say the owner was highly incensed when the matter was reported back to him, and our arrangement was terminated shortly afterwards.

The next year I was able to take a rod on a very pretty stretch of the Dee some way further downstream from the first one. After two years this was given up, the problem being the distance to it from Lake Vyrnwy. So few people were prepared to undertake the car journey of about an hour on twisting roads to reach the river that our rod was hardly ever taken up. Among the few who went there only one succeeded on hooking and losing a salmon: the others all had blank days. From these two examples it can be seen that there are plenty of problems connected with taking fishing for hotel guests from other people.

Turning to shooting, there are various ways in which hotels can arrange this sport for their guests. Some operate schemes whereby they take most of the days on a neighbouring estate each season. Others take odd days on a variety of estates, while there are those who merely put their customers in touch with shoot owners, and leave them to make their own plans. As with taking fishing for guests, there are pitfalls in arranging shooting days for them, as my own limited experience has taught me. Before the days when the Lake Vyrnwy shoot was built up towards its present size I was occasionally asked to find days for parties of guns who could not be accommodated on our own land. On most occasions I was able to do this satisfactorily enough, and both the shoot owners and the parties I sent to them reported that they were satisfied with their parts in the arrangements. Once or twice, however things did not work out so well, as the following two brief stories will show.

The most embarrassing incident involved a group about which I should have been more suspicious after reading the letters of the man organising the visit. They were semi-illiterate and full of silly jokes. On the night of their arrival all members of the party sat up very late drinking heavily, and so set off late the next morning. When they reached the beautiful estate where I had laid on their shooting for them it was discovered that one man had left his gun behind. The keeper very kindly lent him his. Although they were mostly reasonably good shots, and more importantly safe, the owner of the estate was glad when the day drew to a close, and he could prepare to say good-bye to these guns I had wished on him. When they eventually departed insult was added to injury by the head keeper being given just £10 from the whole party, and the man who had borrowed his gun leaving it leaning against a wall, and failing even to say thank-you for the loan. Needless to say the party was told that it would not be welcome for another visit. Fortunately the landowner concerned accepted my apologies with a good grace, but I had learnt a lesson about vetting people before sending them to afflict good neighbours.

On another occasion the fault lay with the hosts. At one point during an otherwise happy day on a Shropshire shoot one of the guns was accused by the keeper of firing a low shot into a wood. No damage was done, and nobody was hurt. Instead of justifiably having a quiet word with the leader of the party at the end of the drive, the keeper came rushing out of the wood in a state bordering on frenzy and shouted obscenities at the amazed line of guns. The day ended on a very sour note, with a far from happy party arriving back at Lake Vyrnwy in the evening.

These two brief accounts of how events that I laid on went wrong serve to show some of the pitfalls awaiting a hotel owner or manager who has to take shooting days for his clients from other people. I must repeat, however, that with care and good luck it is possible to make very satisfactory arrangements. Above all, the motto must be 'leave nothing to chance'.

# CHAPTER TEN

## The Essentials of Hotel Management

Once again the contents of this chapter reflect a purely personal point of view, based on the limited experience of one hotel. Like many other people to be found involved in running places of a similar character in rural locations, I entered the business with little idea of what life would really be like. I envisaged a much more tranquil and unhurried existence than it was ever possible to achieve, and anticipated having time for my other interests to an extent which never materialised. In spite of a certain disillusionment when I discovered the true nature of a hotel proprietor's daily round, I found the work interesting, and for much of the time enjoyable as well. As my partner Ruth Moir once said: 'If you enjoy 75% of what you are doing in life, you are getting along pretty well.' I was lucky enough to be 75% satisfied.

I do not think my lack of professional training in hotel management was any disadvantage. You do not need a PhD to run a good pub: what you need is a clear understanding of the essentials which are described below. However, before describing them, certain obvious matters must be mentioned which are probably self-evident. There is a well-known saying that the three prime requisites for a successful hotel are: 'Site, site, and site.' Certainly one established in an unsuitable location will never be a success, however well run, so being situated in the right place is a first essential. Other obvious requirements include adequate warmth; plenty of hot water; pleasant, though not necessarily luxurious, interior decoration; and in modern times bedrooms with their own private bath-rooms and lavatories. All sections of the building and its contents, needless to say, must be kept thoroughly clean.

Assuming that all these requirements have been met, there

are three vital factors which decide whether a hotel is a really good one or just run-of-the-mill. These are (not in order of priority as all are of equal importance) the efficiency of the reception system, the standard of the food, and the manners of the staff.

It took me a very long time to realise the importance of the reception system, which covers all aspects of a guest's contact with a hotel from a first tentative telephone call to handing over a bill, and saying good-bye, at the end of a visit. It was a charming German lady travel writer who brought home to me in conversation the significance of this aspect. She pointed out that a person who had been received on arrival with a really efficient and friendly welcome would excuse almost any fault in a hotel, while nothing would be right for someone whose arrival had been met with muddle or surly indifference. While it is easy to point out this irrefutable fact, it is not quite so simple to ensure that a reception office is always able to handle matters correctly.

The first problem is concerned with time. Guests require attention from, say, 7 am until about 11 pm even in a country hotel. To have efficient, properly rested people on duty for 16 hours a day is a considerable strain on the resources of even a large, urban establishment: for a small to medium-size place in a rural area it is a constant problem. Apart from finding the people to do the work satisfactorily, the long period to be covered each day means that paying those who can be found is expensive. If expense is avoided by trusting to anyone who is available to answer telephones or meet arrivals, there is always the risk of failing to provide that standard of welcome which has just been shown to be so vital.

Handling telephone enquiries is much more complicated than it might appear. To start with, a caller expects a reasonably quick response, and if one does not come after a long series of rings he or she may give up in disgust, and a valuable bit of business may be lost. Indeed, the opportunities to lose good bookings by inefficient answering of the telephone are much greater than might be imagined. To avoid such slips, the person taking a call must answer swiftly and politely; must be able to give availability of rooms and prices without too much delay; and must remember to record all necessary information about the customer's own details and exact requirements. While reservations by letter are more satisfactory, there is often not time for these, nor even to write in confirmation of a telephone booking, so what is dealt with verbally must avoid all error. This is much easier said than done.

In looking after the guest while actually staying in a hotel, the people working in the reception area will have many odd things to do which cannot be elaborated upon here, but are generally obvious. At the end of the stay comes the moment most fraught with the possibility of destroying a heretofore pleasant relationship – the presentation of the bill. Errors in favour of the hotel are usually noticed immediately, while those in favour of the customer sometimes go unmarked. Those most often found in the former category include failure to record a deposit made in advance, or charging a rate different to one originally quoted. Having to apologise for such errors, and correct them, is a galling business, which has to be done with the best grace possible while inwardly cursing oneself or one's staff for being so stupid.

There is no need to give further examples of ways in which a first-class reception system is of such consequence in running a good hotel. It took me a long time to wake up to this obvious fact, and I suspect many proprietors and managers around the country never do so. It must be remembered, however, that it is far from easy to achieve, and must be constantly worked at. In this respect it has much in common with the next essential to discuss, which is the maintenance of a good standard of food.

In catering the key word is consistency, not with reference to the texture of the product, but in respect of its quality, and the promptitude with which it is served. My personal preference is for simple meals, and I believe that a country hotel does best to stick to uncomplicated menus of straightforward, traditional dishes. Apart from the fact that I would far rather be offered a short menu of simple choices than be handed an elaborate bill of fare expressed in high-flown, fancy language, there are many advantages in being slightly unsophisticated. It is much more likely that a limited number of dishes will be really well cooked and flavoured than will be the case if a big selection is offered. While not necessarily the case, and there are clearly examples where this statement does not apply, the facilities of the average country hotel favour a restricted number of alternatives. What is more, it is possible to ensure that the guests being served with the food can receive each course without undue delay.

The strain of providing first-class meals at regular intervals throughout the day on seven days a week, and of ensuring that they are deftly and pleasantly served, should never be underestimated. Because of this strain, it is wise to avoid being over-ambitious, but to concentrate on supplying a consistent standard of meals at the best level the hotel's facilities will allow. The situation has been eased to some extent in recent years as the demand for luncheons of three or more courses has virtually disappeared, except for people celebrating some special event. The provision of a simple cold buffet, or bar meals, is now generally considered adequate in a country hotel. Many guests will probably want picnic lunches, and although the preparation of these takes the strain off the kitchen, it requires a good deal of effort and imagination to come up with a really attractive end product. Where there is always a big demand for picnics no short cuts should be taken in preparing them.

What to do about tea is a problem. Some places do not provide it at all these days, some only provide tea and biscuits, while a few still offer a traditional full spread of toast, sandwiches, cake and so on. The value of serving teas is to be found in terms of goodwill rather than for any financial gain. The sort of prices that can be charged are never sufficient to cover the cost of preparing teas and paying staff to serve them, but every now and then new guests will return to stay as residents having originally been inspired by a short visit just for tea.

The two meals at which a hotel must maintain the highest possible standards are breakfast and dinner. The temptation to cut corners over arrangements for breakfast is all too often resisted less fiercely than it should be. A certain amount of self-service from a well set up side-board is acceptable, but thin, tinned fruit juice and butter and marmalade in horrible little plastic containers are most certainly not. To cook and serve delicious, substantial breakfasts is just as demanding a task as providing any other meal, requiring as much, if not more, attention to detail.

In discussing dinner, the first thing to establish is the difference between a restaurant and a hotel dining-room. Usually the former goes with a large establishment in an urban or suburban setting, and deliberately encourages the presence of customers other than residents. The latter, while usually open to non-residents, is geared to the requirements of people staying in the hotel, and is what is normally found in places in country settings. A restaurant will probably serve dinner from 7 to 10 pm, and will offer both a set and an à la carte menu. The staff running it will work under different conditions to those involved in a dining-room, where dinner will be available for a much shorter period of time, and on a much less extensive scale. My own personal experience relates only to a dining-room, where dinner was served at a set time. I believe this to be the most suitable arrangement for a small place in a rural area, especially when local staff from the surrounding neighbourhood are employed.

In respect of the menu provided in a dining-room, I return to the earlier plea for simplicity, and suggest a series of choices in threes. To start soup, pâté, and one other alternative; next one red meat dish, one of white meat, and one of fish; then three types of pudding; and finally three English and three French cheeses on a board. To send in a well cooked dinner in this range of variety is enough to tax the skill of any chef or cook working with limited assistance and facilities.

Having expressed these personal preferences, I must admit that the restaurant now operating at Lake Vrynwy provides dinners of outstanding quality, which I am always hearing praised in glowing terms, both by residents and casual visitors. Jim Talbot's expertise as a restaurateur, backed by the skills of head chef Andy Wood and his assistant Noreen Williams, produce exceptional results. They are, however, an exceptional team, and their unusual range of ability is unlikely to be found in the average country hotel. For this reason, I still believe that running a dining-room with a simple range of menus is the best answer for most such establishments.

As important as the quality of the food is the way in which it is served, which brings me to the third of the three vital factors mentioned at the start of the chapter, namely the manners of the staff. The ideal to be sought after is the creation of an unhurried atmosphere of quiet efficiency, in which all the guests' requirements are met with a cheerful willingness and a minimum of fuss. To get the correct balance, so that annoying over attentiveness or excessive obsequiousness are avoided, and yet there is no hint of carelessness or undue familiarity, is something which must be worked at constantly. The lead must come from the top, with the owner or manager personally demonstrating the correct attitude towards the guests, and also watching to ensure that the staff follow his or her example. As far as possible, everyone should enjoy doing the job well. The right outlook for those working in the hotel business at all levels was well described in a television programme I once saw about a man who was starting up a new country pub. Talking to his newly recruited staff just before the opening day he told them that he wanted their jobs to be fun for them, stressing at the same time: 'Fun, but not a joke.' It makes a useful motto for engendering the right spirit into the staff of any hotel, but is especially valuable in relation to a small, rural establishment where a friendly atmosphere is so essential.

Inevitably an explanation of these three important aspects of hotel management sounds trite, and obvious, when set down in this way. However, though there may be nothing very original in what I have written, I can guarantee that any hotel which provides a warm welcome, consistently good, simple food, and well-mannered service will never fail to have plenty of satisfied customers.

# APPENDIX 'A'

Record of Trout Caught in the Lake from 1890 to 1991

| YEAR | TOTAL | WEIGHT | AVERAGE | REMARKS |
|---|---|---|---|---|
| 1891 | 4,143 | 3,664 lb | 14 oz | Fishing started with a trial week in early February with four rods out. Initial indications most encouraging. |
| 1892 | 2,950 | 1,620 lb | 10 oz | Best fish taken in year was 2 lb 6 oz by Capt. G. H. France. The fish was 18½ inches long. |
| 1893 | 4,340 | 2,791 lb | 10¼ oz | Best fish was 2 lb 12 oz in May. Still many trout of over the pound being killed. |
| 1894 | 2,850 | 1,829 | 9½ oz | One notable entry was for 3 September: 'Boatmen. 15 fish of total 12 lb for Duke of York's Luncheon.' |
| 1895 | 1,773 | 1,131 lb | 10 oz | Best flies quoted as 'Zulu and Claret and Mallard'. |
| 1896 | 2,093 | 1,312 lb | 11 oz | |
| 1897 | 2,767 | 1,916 lb | 11 oz | |
| 1898 | 3,348 | 2,397 lb | 11½ oz | Note: 'Chubbing started today. Killed 1,300 fish weighing one ton.' Entry Tuesday, 14 June. |
| 1899 | 3,274 | 2,079 lb | 10 oz | Record bag for Lake so far of 43 fish, 27 lb, by Rev Gregorie and boatman. |
| 1900 | 2,474 | 1,757 lb | 11½ oz | Mr Garside caught 45 fish, 38 lb 'best yet made on Lake'. |
| 1901 | 2,871 | 1,916 lb | 10½ oz | |
| 1902 | 3,120 | 2,127 lb | 11 oz | |
| 1903 | 3,789 | 2,813 lb | 12 oz | |
| 1904 | 3,615 | 2,694 lb | 11½ oz | |
| 1905 | 2,724 | 1,902 lb | 11 oz | |

| YEAR | TOTAL | WEIGHT | AVERAGE | REMARKS |
|---|---|---|---|---|
| 1906 | 2,144 | | 7¾ oz | |
| 1907 | 2,559 | | 8 oz | |
| 1908 | 2,654 | | 8 oz | |
| 1909 | 2,599 | | 8¼ oz | |
| 1910 | 3,932 | | 8½ oz | |
| 1911 | 4,050 | | | |
| 1912 | 3,989 | | 8 oz | |
| 1913 | 4,545 | 2,348 lb | 8 oz | |
| 1914 | 2,752 | 1,366 lb | 8 oz | 1 August – 'Fishing closed owing to Great European War'. |
| 1915 | 2,860 | | 8 oz | |
| 1916 | 2,157 | 1,127 lb | 8½ oz | |
| 1917 | 2,458 | 1,265 | 8½ oz | |
| 1918 | 3,590 | 1,725 lb | 8 oz | Weight and numbers include some River fish. |
| 1919 | 2,152 | 1,034 lb | 8 oz | |
| 1920 | 1,607 | 735 lb | 7½ oz | |
| 1921 | 1,399 | 700 lb | 8 oz | 'These figs. not reliable.' |
| 1922 | 2,077 | 939 lb | 7½ oz | |
| 1923 | 2,217 | 1,049 lb | 7½ oz | |
| 1924 | 2,788 | 1,356 lb | 8 oz | |
| 1925 | 2,503 | 1,204 lb | 8 oz | |
| 1926 | 2,634 | 1,313 lb | 8 oz | |
| 1927 | 3,910 | 1,930 lb | 8 oz | |
| 1928 | 2,551 | 1,189 lb | 8 oz | |
| 1929 | 3,394 | 1,565 lb | 8 oz | Stocking started. Introduction of 'limit'. |
| 1930 | 3,429 | 1,698 lb | 8 oz | Extra feed for fish introduced into Lake. 100,000 Limnea Peregra and 20,000 Gammarus laid down in bays. |
| 1931 | 3,836 | 1,863 lb | 8 oz | |
| 1932 | 2,900 | 1,217 lb | 8 oz | 9 inch limit still in force since 1929. |
| 1933 | 3,311 | 1,537 lb | 8 oz | Lake at lowest since first filled in June. |
| 1934 | 5,902 | 3,570 lb | 10 oz | '50,000 shrimps and snails introduced as extra feed.' |
| 1935 | 4,853 | 3,111 lb | 10 oz | |
| 1936 | 5,493 | 4,145 lb | 12½ oz | Nine Rainbows of over 3 lb taken during the year. |
| 1937 | 4,467 | 3,377 lb | | |
| 1938 | 3,901 | 2,881 lb | 12 oz | |
| 1939 | 3,022 | 2,497 lb | 13 oz | |
| 1940 | 2,674 | | | |

| YEAR | TOTAL | WEIGHT | AVERAGE | REMARKS |
|---|---|---|---|---|
| 1941 | 2,487 | | | Due to the Second World War, there was no stocking of fish between the end of 1940 and spring 1943. Transport being the obvious problem. Soldiers may have taken a considerable number of other fish. |
| 1942 | 1,607 | | | |
| 1943 | 2,502 | | | |
| 1944 | 1,403 | | | |
| 1945 | 2,155 | | | |
| 1946 | 1,929 | 781 lb | 6½ oz | |
| 1947 | 1,626 | 692 lb | 7 oz | |
| 1948 | 1,369 | 622 lb | 7 oz | |
| 1949 | 1,266 | 614 lb | 7¾ oz | |
| 1950 | 1,317 | 561 lb | 7 oz | |
| 1951 | 1,450 | 610 lb | 6¾ oz | |
| 1952 | 1,830 | 832 lb | 7½ oz | Fish of 3 lb 13 oz taken by Col. Page near the Tower. The biggest trout out of the Lake for over 30 years. |
| 1953 | 1,478 | 705 lb | 7½ oz | Mr F. Ledsam took a fish of 4 lb 10 oz. Length 23 inches, girth 13 inches. Biggest trout taken from the fishery since it started in 1891. |
| 1954 | 1,824 | 895 lb | 8 oz | |
| 1955 | 1,286 | 693 lb | 8½ oz | |
| 1956 | 1,817 | 896 lb | 8 oz | |
| 1957 | 1,810 | 920 lb | 8 oz | Average weight still just on the half pound mark – although a small increase in size noticeable. |
| 1958 | 1,564 | 824 lb | 8½ oz | |
| 1959 | 1,417 | 738 lb | 8½ oz | The extraordinary dry summer brought drought to the Vyrnwy watershed. The lake reached its lowest level since initial flooding in the late 1880s. |
| 1960 | 1,646 | 872 lb | 8 oz | Water level fully recovered. |
| 1961 | 1,811 | 1,012 lb | 9 oz | |
| 1962 | 1,127 | 611 lb | 9 oz | |
| 1963 | 908 | 522 lb | 8½ oz | |
| 1964 | 1,304 | 732 lb | 9 oz | |
| 1965 | 1,205 | 634 lb | 8½ oz | |

| YEAR | TOTAL | WEIGHT | AVERAGE | | | REMARKS |
|---|---|---|---|---|---|---|
| 1966 | 1,162 | 618 lb | 8½ oz | | | Brook trout first introduced as an experiment. Only 29 taken in season out of 250 entered. |
| 1967 | 1,397 | 725 lb | 8½ oz | | | A further 37 Brook trout taken. |
| 1968 | 1,203 | 657 lb | 9 oz | | | Record – but unrecorded – fish of 7 lb 2 oz taken by Mr Norman Davies in June 1968 just below Cedig. Certainly the largest out of lake to date. |
| 1969 | 995 | 557 lb | 9 oz | | | |
| 1970 | 1,193 | 675 lb | 9 oz | | | |
| 1971 | 1,233 | 712 lb | 9½ oz | | | |
| 1972 | 989 | 609 lb | 10 oz | | | |
| 1973 | 1,614 | 1,387 227 | brown rainbow | 1,122 lb | 14 oz | First year with rainbows entered for a long time 425 put in and 227 caught. |
| 1974 | 1,623 | 1,235 388 | brown rainbow | 1,151 lb | 11 oz | Michael Ledger took 20 trout on 18 May. Last basket of 20 since that date. |
| 1975 | 1,451 | 944 507 | brown rainbow | 1,151 lb | 13 oz | 970 rainbows entered, the biggest number since pre-war. Total stocking was 1,770 trout, but return looks poor because some of these were only 8 inches. |
| 1976 | 1,357 | 1,031 326 | brown rainbow | 1,124 lb | 14 oz | The year of the drought. Only 180 trout taken in all in July, August and September. |
| 1977 | 1,859 | 1,613 245 | brown rainbow | 1,539 lb | 14 oz | Best year since 1948. |
| 1978 | 1,787 | 1,458 329 | brown rainbow | 1,772 lb | 1 lb | Average weight reached 1 lb for the first time in the history of the Lake Vyrnwy fishery. |

| YEAR | TOTAL | WEIGHT | | AVERAGE | | REMARKS |
|---|---|---|---|---|---|---|
| 1979 | 2,101 | 1,610 | brown | 2,032 lb | 15½ oz | 36 trout over 2½ lbs in season. Biggest fish 5½ lbs brown. |
| | | 491 | rainbow | | | |
| | | - | brook | | | |
| 1980 | 2,050 | 1,454 | brown | 1,788 lb | 13½ oz | Biggest fish 3¼ lbs brown. |
| | | 527 | rainbow | | | |
| | | 60 | brook | | | |
| 1981 | 2,525 | 1,646 | brown | 2,232 lb | 14½ oz | Best season for many years. Biggest fish 3¾ brown. |
| | | 511 | rainbow | | | |
| | | 368 | brook | | | |
| 1982 | 2,211 | 1,332 | brown | 1,839 lb | 13 oz | Biggest fish 4½ lbs brown. |
| | | 479 | rainbow | | | |
| | | 400 | brook | | | |
| 1983 | 2,423 | 1,514 | brown | 2,093 lb | 13½ oz | Biggest fish 3¼ lbs rainbow. |
| | | 575 | rainbow | | | |
| | | 334 | brook | | | |
| 1984 | 2,174 | 1,255 | brown | 2,106 lb | 15½ oz | Biggest fish 3½ lbs rainbow. |
| | | 666 | rainbow | | | |
| | | 253 | brook | | | |
| 1985 | 2,234 | 1,671 | brown | 2,237 lb | 1 lb | Average over 1 lb. Biggest fish 3½ lbs rainbow. |
| | | 413 | rainbow | | | |
| | | 120 | brook | | | |
| 1986 | 1,496 | 1,172 | brown | 1,356 lb | 15 oz | Very bad weather in April and March. Biggest fish 4 lb 14 oz rainbow. |
| | | 323 | rainbow | | | |
| | | 1 | brook | | | |
| 1987 | 2,451 | - | brown | 2,289 lb | 15 oz | Biggest fish 4¾ lbs brown. |
| | | - | rainbow | | | |
| | | - | brook | | | |
| 1988 | 2,807 | 1,863 | brown | 2,710 lb | 15½ oz | Record trout to date Biggest fish 6¾ lbs brown. |
| | | 805 | rainbow | | | |
| | | 139 | brook | | | |
| 1989 | 2,262 | 1,139 | brown | 2,255 lb | 1 lb | |
| | | 1,038 | rainbow | | | |
| | | 86 | brook | | | |
| 1990 | 2,057 | 1,033 | brown | 2,068 lb | 1 lb | |
| | | 1,023 | rainbow | | | |
| | | 1 | brook | | | |
| 1991 | 2,958 | 1,821 | brown | 2,832 lb | 15½ oz | Best total since 1939 Biggest fish 7 lbs 2 oz rainbow. Record for the lake. |
| | | 1,137 | rainbow | | | |
| | | - | brook | | | |

# APPENDIX 'B'

## Record of Game Shot
## 1890–1928

1890–1914　Average bag of grouse for the season during these years was 1,600 (800 brace)

1914–1928　Exact totals not known, except that the bag in 1917 was 710.

## 1929–1946

| Year | Grouse (birds, not brace) | Pheasants (where known) | Remarks |
|---|---|---|---|
| 1929 | 876 | — | |
| 1930 | 773 | 86 | W. R. Bull arrived as keeper |
| 1931 | 629 | 282 | G. Martin started to build up |
| 1932 | 589 | 773 | the shoot |
| 1933 | 554 | 1,202 | |
| 1934 | 515 | 1,912 | Biggest day - 412 pheasants |
| 1935 | 644 | 1,324 | |
| 1936 | 755 | 1,825 | |
| 1937 | 814 | 1,733 | T. Hughes retired as head |
| 1938 | 639 | 1,454 | moor keeper |
| 1939 | 297 | 291 | Outbreak of war |
| 1940 | 135 | — | |
| 1941 | 99 | — | |
| 1942 | 46 | — | |
| 1943 | 26 | — | |
| 1944 | 34 | — | |
| 1945 | — | — | |
| 1946 | — | — | |

## 1947–1992

| Season | Grouse | Black Game | Partridges | Pheasants | Wood-cock | Snipe | Wild-fowl | Wood Pigeon | Hares | Rabbits | Various | Total |
|---|---|---|---|---|---|---|---|---|---|---|---|---|
| 1947/48 | 10 | 5 | 6 | 9 | 1 | 7 | 11 | 17 | 2 | 161 | 15 | 244 |
| 1948/49 | 19 | — | 9 | 28 | 5 | 15 | 3 | 5 | 8 | 440 | 6 | 538 |
| 1949/50 | 29 | — | 11 | 43 | 2 | 16 | 4 | 14 | 13 | 623 | 3 | 758 |
| 1950/51 | 21 | 2 | 60 | 86 | — | 32 | 6 | 2 | 13 | 777 | — | 999 |
| 1951/52 | 81 | — | 67 | 119 | 4 | 41 | 5 | 21 | 14 | 736 | 9 | 1,097 |
| 1952/53 | 72 | — | 65 | 109 | 1 | 16 | 14 | 34 | 18 | 537 | 7 | 873 |
| 1953/54 | 101 | — | 48 | 135 | 6 | 29 | 7 | 45 | 3 | 389 | 30 | 793 |
| 1954/55 | 66 | — | 6 | 117 | 3 | 8 | 3 | 25 | 7 | 229 | — | 464 |
| 1955/56 | 72 | — | 2 | 50 | 1 | 7 | 1 | — | 1 | — | 1 | 135 |
| 1956/57 | 77 | — | — | 54 | 1 | — | 8 | — | 1 | — | 1 | 142 |
| 1957/58 | 129 | — | — | 72 | 2 | 3 | 5 | 8 | 5 | — | 1 | 225 |
| 1958/59 | 75 | — | — | 59 | 2 | 3 | 7 | 2 | 5 | — | — | 153 |
| 1959/60 | 132 | — | — | 64 | 5 | 3 | 3 | 13 | 21 | 5 | 3 | 249 |
| 1960/61 | 102 | — | — | 65 | 1 | 2 | 1 | 47 | 15 | 5 | — | 238 |
| 1961/62 | 72 | — | — | 42 | 3 | — | — | 22 | 6 | 2 | 2 | 149 |
| 1962/63 | 45 | 2 | — | 28 | 2 | — | — | 83 | 4 | 5 | 1 | 170 |
| 1963/64 | 72 | 7 | 1 | 67 | 4 | — | 5 | 22 | 6 | 8 | 1 | 107 |
| 1964/65 | 82 | 2 | — | 42 | 1 | — | — | 6 | 2 | 19 | — | 154 |
| 1965/66 | 134 | 5 | — | 22 | 1 | 2 | — | 30 | 3 | — | 3 | 200 |
| 1966/67 | 173 | 5 | — | 35 | 2 | 1 | 2 | 33 | — | 61 | — | 312 |
| 1967/68 | 92 | — | — | 44 | — | — | 5 | 143 | 1 | 39 | 4 | 328 |
| 1968/69 | 100 | — | — | 27 | — | — | — | 96 | 2 | 33 | — | 258 |
| 1969/70 | 98 | — | — | 50 | — | — | 5 | 67 | — | — | 1 | 221 |
| 1970/71 | 178 | 1 | — | 34 | 2 | 3 | 2 | 1 | 1 | 5 | 4 | 231 |
| 1971/72 | 100 | — | — | 23 | 1 | — | — | 44 | 1 | — | — | 169 |
| 1972/73 | 177 | — | — | 29 | 2 | 1 | — | 19 | — | — | 2 | 230 |
| 1973/74 | 223 | 1 | — | 47 | — | 4 | — | 1 | 3 | — | — | 279 |
| 1974/75 | 171 | 1 | — | 71 | — | 4 | 1 | 1 | — | — | — | 249 |
| 1975/76 | 180 | — | — | 130 | 4 | 6 | 7 | — | — | — | 1 | 328 |
| 1976/77 | 173 | 1 | 2 | 144 | 3 | 3 | 9 | 1 | 3 | 3 | 1 | 343 |
| 1977/78 | 128 | — | — | 207 | 2 | — | 44 | 1 | 1 | — | — | 383 |
| 1978/79 | 93 | — | — | 279 | 6 | 2 | 40 | — | — | — | 1 | 421 |
| 1979/80 | 79 | — | — | 346 | 10 | — | 12 | — | 2 | — | — | 449 |
| 1980/81 | 73 | — | — | 442 | 9 | 1 | 39 | 1 | — | 1 | — | 566 |
| 1981/82 | 52 | — | — | 473 | 5 | 1 | 72 | 3 | — | — | — | 606 |
| 1982/83 | 47 | — | — | 669 | 4 | — | 86 | 5 | 1 | — | — | 812 |
| 1983/84 | 14 | — | — | 842 | 7 | — | 96 | 1 | 4 | — | — | 964 |
| 1984/85 | 48 | 1 | — | 1,008 | 15 | 1 | 146 | 3 | 5 | 5 | — | 1,232 |
| 1985/86 | 51 | — | — | 1,313 | 9 | — | 161 | — | 3 | — | — | 1,537 |
| 1986/87 | 26 | — | — | 1,156 | 14 | — | 166 | — | 1 | 1 | — | 1,364 |
| 1987/88 | 14 | — | 16 | 3,026 | 8 | 1 | 216 | 3 | — | — | — | 3,284 |
| 1988/89 | 7 | — | 21 | 4,620 | 17 | 8 | 238 | — | 7 | — | 5 | 4,923 |
| 1989/90 | 12 | — | — | 5,000 | 21 | 1 | 177 | — | 1 | 1 | 4 | 5,220 |
| 1990/91 | 33 | — | — | 4,523 | 33 | — | 48 | 5 | 2 | — | 2 | 4,646 |
| 1991/92 | 24 | — | — | 4,653 | 15 | — | 7 | 1 | 1 | 5 | — | 4,706 |